JOURNEY TO THE DARK GODDESS

Five thousand years ago, Inanna, the Queen of Heaven and Earth, dares to journey to meet Ereshkigal, the Queen of the Underworld. Jane Meredith wisely guides us today on this crucial, mysterious and challenging journey (the descent and the ascent) that every one of us must take as part of our initiation into becoming human. The reward is to know our selves and so, to be able to care for others. This is a wise, wonderful and inspiring book. Thank you, Jane.

Diane Wolkstein, Author, *Inanna: Queen of Heaven and Earth: Her Stories and Hymns from Sumer*

Jane Meredith is a wise, compassionate guide who teaches women to approach their experiences of loss, darkness and death as sacred initiations. Filled with practical advice and rituals *Journey to the Dark Goddess* shows how, by following in the footsteps of ancient Goddesses, we can emerge radiant and whole from the dark realms of the underworld.

Jalaja Bonheim, Ph.D, author of *Aphrodite's Daughters: Women's Sexual Stories and the Journey of the Soul*

Journey to the Dark Goddess provides a clear and profound psychological map for women journeying into their depths. For some the underworld comes unbidden to us through life's circumstances, for others it can be an exploration entered into deliberately to seek wisdom and transformation. However we make the descent, Jane Meredith's unique mix of therapeutic storytelling, exercises and creative activities facilitate a productive and powerful venture into the realms of the Dark Goddess. I recommend it for anyone wishing to explore their shadow and reclaim their personal power.

Ali Harrison, Transpersonal Psychotherapist

Interesting insights, creative ideas and conscious rituals all designed to help you understand the experiences you might have during a Journey of Descent into the Dark Goddess' realm, while you are held there in Her Underworld, and as you Ascend out of the Underworld, returning once again to the surface of your life.

I recommend this book to all who are entering into the Underworld, either consciously by design or by falling into Her world unexpectedly and unaware.

Kathy Jones, Organizer of the Glastonbury Goddess Conference, author of *Priestess of Avalon, Priestess of the Goddess*

Like others before her, Meredith challenges the reader to face the darkness within themselves and within nature more broadly. That her challenge is so comprehensive makes this a book worth reading.

Emma Restall Orr, Author of *Kissing the Hag*

Journey to the Dark Goddess:

How to Return to Your Soul

Journey to the Dark Goddess:

How to Return to Your Soul

Jane Meredith

MOON

BOOKS

Winchester, UK
Washington, USA

First published by Moon Books, 2012
Moon Books is an imprint of John Hunt Publishing Ltd., Laurel House, Station Approach,
Alresford, Hants, SO24 9JH, UK
office1@jhpbooks.net
www.johnhuntpublishing.com
www.moon-books.net

For distributor details and how to order please visit the 'Ordering' section on our website.

Text copyright: Jane Meredith 2011

ISBN: 978 1 84694 677 6

A CIP catalogue record for this book is available from the British Library.

Design: Stuart Davies

Printed in the UK by CPI Antony Rowe

We operate a distinctive and ethical publishing philosophy in all
areas of our business, from our global network of authors to
production and worldwide distribution.

CONTENTS

DEDICATION

This book is dedicated to the Dark Goddess,
and her mysteries.
Ereshkigal, Persephone, Hecate, Kali, Morgana,
Black Isis, Lilith...

JOURNEY TO THE DARK GODDESS

The Dark Goddess is a mysterious and hidden figure. Although each of us is familiar with her roles of wicked witch, the crone, the bad mother, the hag and the winter queen, we don't always remember her other face of compassion, healing and rebirth. This does us a great disservice. It leaves us disconnected from the full range of the feminine divine and estranged from much of our ability to change and grow. In a journey to the Dark Goddess we travel deeply into ourselves, seeking answers to difficulties, strength in a crisis, and healing or change when we have become stuck. Sometimes we make this journey consciously, but all too often we find ourselves on the path without knowing how we got there, what to do or how to get out. Some of us spend years down there, in a shadowy, inner realm known as the Underworld.

Each journey to the Dark Goddess is different, yet the pattern of journeys remains the same. They begin with an awareness, a feeling that something in our lives is not quite right. When this awareness arises we may set off to investigate it. But often we don't. Often we prefer to ignore that awareness, that small voice, that feeling of something awry; and we're capable of ignoring it for quite a long time. Eventually it gets too much and all of a sudden we are swamped; collapsing under stress, illness, emotional crisis, overwork or an outright disbelief that this could be our life. Then, as everything falls apart around us, we are forced to begin the search for understanding and change.

When we undertake a journey towards the Dark Goddess much that we have accumulated is stripped away. Sometimes we experience this as having parts of our lives we have relied on taken from us; such as health, relationships, emotional stability and status. We cannot visit the Dark Goddess while still keeping our place in the world; we cannot be in two places at once. This means we have to strip off – or more painfully, be stripped of – all our guises, props and patterns that are so much a part of our lives we have almost come to think of them as ourselves. In stripping down to the core we find our intrinsic self, or our soul and that is where we meet with the Dark Goddess.

Journeying to the Dark Goddess is filled with paradoxes. For an empowering and inspiring experience it is best to travel towards her willingly; yet we almost never do that. If we want to understand the Dark Goddess and the part she plays in our lives we have to invoke her, invite her in, sit with her. Instead we shun, avoid and cower from her. We experience her as utterly other – the scary witch, a faceless dark power, a nightmare – as removed from ourselves as possible; yet when we finally meet with her we discover she is a part of us. And not just any part. We find her in the deepest, truest remnant of our souls; always there to remind us – when we make the journey – of who we are on the inside. One of the paradoxes is that the worst times in our lives – times when we felt out of control, in grief, pain and distress – can be followed by the emergence of new inspiration and energy, accompanied by determination to live a life of beauty and meaning. This is a rebirth by the Dark Goddess.

Our culture has not taught us how to listen to the Dark Goddess, how to journey towards her or how to integrate her wisdom into our lives. But instructions remain in myths from other times and places. Many women have found support and guidance in the stories of the Goddesses. In Greek myths both Persephone and Psyche journey to the Underworld. In Sumerian mythology Inanna (known as Ishtar in Babylon) is famous for her visit to the Dark Goddess. From these stories we can learn much of the journey to the Underworld, and the return.

Journey to the Dark Goddess will focus on feminine myths of descent, although these stories are not feminine alone. Dumuzi, Inanna's lover and consort also journeys to the Underworld; Ishtar's beloved Tammuz dies ritually in her arms every year with the vegetation; and Orpheus journeys into the Underworld in a Greek myth to seek his dead beloved, Eurydice. Closer to home, Jesus Christ lay dead in a cave for three days before rising again. Myths and stories can be read as maps of the unconscious; a Jungian collective unconscious or an individual's psyche. But they are also quite practical maps that tell us – literally – where to go, how to get there and what to do when we get there. And how to get back.

Where do all these myths come from; and how could it be that they share the same basic pattern? Demetra George, in her wonderful book *Mysteries of the Dark Moon* usefully points out that past humans, wherever they were on the planet, shared the same observations of natural life.

People everywhere saw vegetation dying (often in winter), returning to the earth and then rising again. They observed that seeds, buried in the earth, rose up into new life. They saw the days get shorter and colder and then – magically, mystically – turn around and get longer and warmer. They saw the moon, every month, vanish (obliterated from sight, when it is too close to the sun to be seen) for three nights; then to appear again – on the other side of the sun. Reborn, you might say. These observations are blueprints of the myths and explain why so many cultures and religions share this story of death and resurrection – a journey to an impossible, almost unimagined place where something mysterious happens which leads to a return.

All cultures have seen what we still see today; that humans are born, grow, get old and die; and that new humans, meanwhile, are born. The death part, or disappearing into the Underworld is still mysterious and unknown but we can clearly see, from the moon, the seasons and the sun that the return will occur. If the return is in a body other than our own (our children's, or grand-children's or simply other members of our tribe or village), surely that only deepens the mystery. A basic law of visits to the Underworld is that you return changed.

The Underworld gets some bad press. We associate it with helplessness, pain, fear, depression and despair. This is at least partly because we so strongly resist and delay visiting these dark and difficult places of confronting the truth of our lives. We have a backlog to deal with, when we are finally forced into it. This bad press is due to our unfamiliarity with the terrain, and to underlying values and beliefs our culture holds such as *growth is good, diminishment is bad* and *staying in control is necessary at all times*. We know these values depict only half the story. Of course diminishment is necessary, of course we are not in control of even the main cornerstones of our own lives, being born and dying; but it is still very hard to force ourselves to act from a different basis.

Journeying to the Dark Goddess changes us, each time we undertake that journey. To prepare to visit the Dark Goddess we have to stop and listen to ourselves; deeply. We have to admit to the parts of our lives that are not working, that are making us unhappy or even ill and we have to be prepared to do something about them. To descend into the Underworld we have to give away, one by one, all the things that hold us back from change. This can feel like we are losing everything. Meeting the Dark Goddess herself is at the heart of the mystery and is different each time, but that is the point where change happens. The return journey – that of the Ascent – is the time when we put those changes into action, integrating what we have learnt.

For some women, journeying towards the Dark Goddess is not the issue. Some of us feel like we've spent all or most of our lives with her. We might be artists, healers, mothers and dreamers. But maybe we've also gone through depression; been out of control with addictions or self-harming; or felt balanced on the edge of insanity, unable to escape the Underworld and the immediate and continual presence of the Dark Goddess. When this is happening, learning how to depart from the Underworld is the issue. But these alternatives – barely visiting our hidden selves

4

unless absolutely forced to, or else not being able to get away – are both stories of imbalance. The ancient myths teach of balance; how to visit and how to return. +

The practice of regularly visiting the Underworld helps if you have been running a strong denial, avoidance or fear of the hidden, 'darker' parts of life. It can help if you have felt stuck in the Underworld, unwillingly dedicated to the Dark Goddess or just past due time to leave. Visiting – and departing – the Underworld is probably essential. It should have been taught to us by the time we began our menstrual cycles, in the company of women, with stories, songs and ritual practices. We would have watched adult women – our mothers, older sisters, grand-mothers and teachers – practicing such things all through our childhoods and we would be proud and excited to be learning those things for ourselves. We didn't get that. But we can learn to give it to ourselves, and each other, and our daughters and the daughters of friends and our students. An essential part of returning is that each time we bring back with us gifts and powers from the Underworld which allow us to live more fully and genuinely.

I have sometimes felt I simply didn't have the muscle power required to deal with the Dark Goddess. But I have also found I can build that muscle power up; exercising, as it were. Practicing stepping into – and out of – and into the dark. The Underworld. Bringing myself face to face with the Dark Goddess. Not once; dozens of times. Regularly, unceasingly, on good days and weeks and months and bad days and weeks and months. Only this practice – this discipline, this dedication – helps to balance out the Underworld with the upper world; helps to allow the Dark Goddess a place in my life without having her take over the whole shop, indefinitely. Of course, she can still do that from time to time. But I have garnered a working relationship with her; my sister.

We all enter into fallow periods in our lives, times of

questioning, of crisis, of not-knowing; times of depression, stagnation, terror and loss. We return from them; changed. Later we enter them again. There is no ceasing of this pattern. And it is by attempting to halt the pattern – to avoid the pain/fear/loss part of it – that we cause the greatest damage to ourselves. Imagine a full moon that never waned. What would the astronomers say to that? How would the seas respond? Imagine a world without winter. When would the culling occur? When would be the quiet time for the seeds, nestled in the earth, to propagate? Or a world that was only winter?

It is not as frightening as it seems, to give oneself over to this pattern of descending and ascending once we fully understand that it is cyclic. The pattern does not get stuck in any one place, but continues like the tides; like birth and death, the waning and waxing moon and the turn of the seasons. When we try to halt it, to keep the pattern in one place this creates enormous difficulties. In stasis we cannot learn or grow very deeply, stuck in one phase of a moving system. Then imbalance occurs so, like a volcano steadily building its ammunition in the darkness, when it erupts the result is devastation.

We need to rebuild the cycle. One of the difficulties with our current shunning of the dying-falling away part of the cycle is the depletion of the earth, as we demand it must always be in crop, and every crop must always be available regardless of season. Another imbalance is the endless demand for economic growth; that the shares index must always move upwards, capital and national growth increase, retailing turn over more money, profits increase year by year. By learning to journey into the Underworld we are beginning to sway the cycle back to the natural one, where light and dark alternate. There are seasons for growth and fullness and seasons for shedding and rest.

Time spent in the Underworld is a valuable and intrinsic part of our development as a human. This is the night time for us, where we rest, recover, dream and rise refreshed. I would even go further, and say all things are not equal, and those times in the Underworld are the *most* valuable. They are the times of renewal, of understanding and of compassion. It is tragic that this is seen as something best avoided, inimical to the bright progression of one's life and deeply undesirable, even unacceptable. The Dark Goddess knows all our secrets. Traveling towards her we reveal and rediscover ourselves. Meeting her, we change and this change reflects a deep truth of who we really are. The Dark Goddess is both more powerful than, and an intrinsic part of each one of us. The aim of our journey is to visit her; her aim is to remake us.

I am deeply indebted to Robin La Trobe for initially guiding me through the Inanna story as a ritual process, twenty plus years ago and thus starting me on my own *Journey to the Dark Goddess*. I thank all the women who have written books about this journey, and those who've sung songs, made paintings and kept the myths alive. I honor and thank all the women who have shared with me portions of their own journeys into the Underworld and their meetings with the Dark Goddess. Without all of this I would not have had the courage or the conviction to write this book.

JANE MEREDITH

PART ONE:

PREPARING FOR DESCENT

PREPARING FOR DESCENT

Listen. What is that, calling within you? What do you hear? Listen.

Silence the world around you. Listen within. Open your inner ear.

What do you hear?

It is a wordless cry, within you. It is a whispered sequence of words you cannot quite catch. It is the sound of your own voice. It is weeping; singing. It is the promise of your power, struggling to be free. It is the invitation of your soul.

Do you hear her calling? She might be a tiny whisper within you – or longing – or doubt. She might be rapping on your door, persistently. She might be shouting in a voice of the tidal wave of change, come to claim you.

You may be driven to take this journey to meet the Dark Goddess by illness; grief; a gradually increasing despair; emotional numbness or a sudden loss. You might be inspired to take it by spiritual insight, your creative journey or by wanting to fulfill your potential. You might find yourself already there; numbed to the world and relationships around you, subsisting on automatic and completely blank about your future, your hopes, your desires, your self.

Choose, then, to journey within.

It will not be like any journey you have ever undertaken. Even if you have been this way many times, it will not be like any journey you have undertaken.

The way will be strange. Dark. Frightening. The more frightening it is, the more you will understand you are on the right path. The only path. All other paths are detours. They lead back to this path. It will be liberating, to finally take these steps. You will be liberated from everything you have been.

It is dark and it will get darker. In the dark, you head towards *the unknown. You will leave markers behind you. They will be the sum of all the things you care about in the world. You will leave behind your children, your dreams, your projects and successes. You will leave behind your heritage. You will leave behind love and human companionship. You will leave your future behind you. This will be a journey into the Underworld.*

There will be warnings, maybe many warnings.

It would be preferable if you would take this medication.

You ought to be happy, you have what you wanted.

Your behavior is too wild/emotional/irrational.

It doesn't matter what you feel; it's better not to say it.

This is how things are. Grow up. Get used to it.

These warnings will reach your old self, but you will be already beyond them.

This journey is not done lightly. It is not a thing of light. Your family, your friends, they will wring their hands and tear their hair and weep at the gates you have passed through, unable to follow you. You will know they are there, somewhere behind you and you will not turn round. They may shout warnings after you, beg you to consider alternatives, beseech you never to leave them. When you emerge – changed – they will see the changes in you, written across your body and face.

Do it once, unwilling and unaware. It will be very slow. But you will eventually stumble out, dazed by the extremities of suffering and priceless gifts. Do it a second time, still unwilling but aware. Slow, but not as slow. Fight it all you like, some part of you knows how to do this; that you have to give way, wait, be gifted, return. The third time, go willing. Go fast. Or the fourth. Or as soon as you possibly can. Only when you journey deliberately, aware and willing, will you meet the Dark Goddess in her full glory. Only then will you have a chance for the depth of transformation she promises. Only then.

The Dark Goddess speaks in a voice we resist much of the time.

You may first become aware of this voice as tiny internal promptings. She whispers intuitions you don't want to hear; warns you about inappropriate choices of jobs and lovers; and tempts you with things you long to do. But the concerns of the Dark Goddess also go much deeper. Hers is that voice reminding you to go back to the art you abandoned in your twenties; to take singing lessons; go dancing; keep a journal. Hers is the voice urging you to toss in the job you hate and go traveling; to break off that safe relationship with someone you've never really loved and open your life to chance; to pursue a career that has no guarantees but dazzles you with longing.

She tells us to run barefoot on the beach under the full moon, to swim naked in the freezing river, to sing loudly whether anyone is listening or not. Many of the things she says go against what we thought we believed. That voice might tell you to put your baby in childcare and go back to work, though you always thought you'd stay home for the first two years; or to take your children traveling, though you used to scorn other parents who didn't put their children's education first. That voice might tell you to move somewhere no-one knows you; to go back to a university degree you abandoned long ago; to pursue a meditation practice or go on a weekend course of self discovery. The Dark Goddess will not be saying things that keep you within your comfort zone.

The voice of the Dark Goddess is the voice of our own soul, calling out within us. It is not the voice of our personality, which we have built up around that soul over many years and become attached to. This personality has attracted – like a shell around the soul – all sorts of manifestations; likes and dislikes, habits and relationships and jobs until we begin to think that is who we are. When that happens the Dark Goddess starts her rumbling. It's easy to ignore, at least for a while. But ignore it for long enough and eventually, like a volcano, she will blow and the landscape will never be the same again. The stronger – and longer – we have ignored her, the more powerful will be the eventual blow-out. Almost all of us have experienced this at least once in our lives; a domino-like collapse of everything that mattered to us. In these explosions relationships, jobs, health, friendships and houses can be lost; overturned in the great need for purging, evolution and (eventual) replenishment. Most of us shudder at the thought of allowing such explosive changes to rip through our lives again.

I believe if we are able to listen to the Dark Goddess regularly, to hear her voice every day and respond to her as an ordinary part of our lives, the disaster, collapse and devastation would hardly ever happen to us. To act this way goes against all our customs, even against most of the teachings of the 'alternative' or 'new age' culture. To honor the Dark Goddess, to listen to her voice (that voice within us that is so hard to shut up), to respect what she has to say and to undertake regular journeys to visit her requires a different way of viewing the world. In this way of seeing we would not expect everything to be continually onward and upward. Rather, we would model ourselves on the earth's patterns, turning from the light of day naturally and gradually to the darkness, going through the dark and emerging again, gradually, once more into the light. We would model ourselves on the seasons, moving from spring to summer to autumn (or fall) to winter and through to spring again. We would model the moon's cycle, moving from full to dark to full.

This level of allowing for the Dark Goddess requires a major shift in our understanding and willingness to engage with the dark; the unknown, the powerful inner forces of soul, mystery and what I am calling the Dark Goddess. It also requires learning the paths or ways into the Underworld; experimenting with ways to approach the Dark Goddess; and an expansion of our tolerance and skills in the areas of life we mainly seek to avoid, deny and minimize. Practice is a key part of this. Most of us wait until we have no choice to venture off the known paths of our lives and explore the unknown. This does us a disservice. It means we are always heading to the Dark Goddess when we are at our weakest, most stressed, distressed and desperate. When we learn to listen to her, to visit her at other times, we discover whole new levels of her realms not previously obvious to us.

The realm of the dark, sometimes called the Underworld, is a place of dormancy, mystery and generation. If we truly respected it the experiences associated with the Dark Goddess – of change, of letting go, of listening to our souls – would come to be a regular part of life, no longer so severe, devastating or frightening. If we accorded the dark its due – and its due is unavoidably half – I believe our lives would be balanced. Half; as day is half and night is the other half. Half; the same amount of time being given to a dark moon as a full moon, or to a waning moon as a waxing moon. Half; like autumn and winter share the year with summer and spring; half for the growing and half for the decaying.

When we adopt this model and became practiced in the art of moving between the 'upper' and 'under' worlds of our lives (outwardly focused and engaged with the world; inwardly focused and listening to our soul) not only does the pattern of light moving into dark, into light again become clear, but also the gradations. We often experience this movement in dramatic (and unpleasant) swings from one to the other, but bringing practice and awareness to this journeying allows us to settle more gently into these transitions; just as the moon takes two weeks to darken, or lighten in small gradations. After all, we do not spend half the month in a dark moon, and half with a full moon. Rather, there are just a few days each of full darkness and full moon, and all the rest of the time is in gradual transition.

When we choose to journey into the Underworld we receive a major benefit not available to those who just fall into it. We get a chance to prepare ourselves. This preparation can take a number of forms, including clarifying our purpose, or intent; becoming aware of the terrain ahead of us; setting up mechanisms of assis-

14

tance or rescue we may need later; and turning our focus deliberately to the inward parts of ourselves. Studying the myths of journeys into the Underworld gives us many valuable clues, signposts and directions. Even before we begin a Descent, we can start learning about the Dark Goddess and the part she has been playing in our lives.

Who is the Dark Goddess?

The Dark Goddess is an aspect of Goddess, of divinity. She can be seen as a sister or 'other half' to the light Goddess, or the one Goddess. She is also acknowledged as an individual aspect of Goddess (the Dark Mother, the Crone, the Goddess of Death, Decay and Transformation), or as one of many many (countless) Goddesses. She has many names in different cultures and throughout history; Kali, Cerridwyn, the Morrigan, Black Annis, Sheela-na-gig, Ereshkigal, Persephone, Medusa and Hecate are a few of them. Sometimes Mary Magdalene is added to that list. You can read about the Dark Goddess in myths from around the world. She is also a recognizable character in a hundred fairy-tales; the Witch, the Ice Queen, the Wicked Stepmother.

The Dark Goddess can also be understood as being a split-off part of yourself; often the powerful, dangerous part. This aspect functions as an initiator into progressive layers of your depths or, more simply put, your soul. She is the hidden, ruthless part that brings transformation, whether we will or no; the one who propels us through the hardest things. Hers is the voice in the darkest hour and her unflinching honesty and strength can help us to keep going when things are very tough. Her actions – however painfully perceived at the time – culminate not in your death, but in your life.

The Dark Goddess is also a metaphor for meeting our nemesis; the situation or truth that will undo us and our carefully constructed lives. It is an essential aspect of human life that we meet this nemesis, many times. We meet it in our child-

15

hoods; our love-life; giving birth; suffering grief, loss and fear and in witnessing, approaching and contemplating mortality. Meeting our nemesis is an initiation into knowledge, power or a different stage of life. To see her abstractly, the Dark Goddess is for each of us the lessons we need to learn.

The Dark Goddess lives in a special place many mythologies call the Underworld. The Underworld has its own rules, and these are rarely convenient to visitors. The Underworld is literally imagined to be caves, or caverns and in Greek mythology it has a river separating it from the upper world, the river Lethe or the Styx. The Underworld also operates as a metaphor for those times in our lives when we are, to all intents and purposes, *elsewhere*. Life might be going on all around us but we are peculiarly absent from it, emotionally unengaged and watching it almost as if it were someone else's life. The Underworld can also be an intensely inner, focused place we can visit in dreams, in ritual and in meditation. In this place there is no distraction, no untruth and nothing extraneous. It can feel dangerous, liberating or ecstatic. What awaits us there is the essence of our selves, our soul. Calling this the Dark Goddess experience, or viewing it as the domain of the Dark Goddess gives us a way to undertake this journey, as well as lending us divine assistance.

We commonly view the areas of life associated with the Dark Goddess as difficult, painful and unwelcome. Because of this we are not familiar with them, not comfortable treading the paths they require and not adept at working our way through them. Instead we often go down into the realm of the Dark Goddess dramatically; unaware and unprepared. Sometimes it can be years before we even begin to understand what is going on, let alone what we can, or need to do about it. Other times we know perfectly well what to do, but in the face of little or no support – or sometimes actual obstacles placed in our way – it takes a very long time and much suffering to emerge out the other side. I have watched women trying to come off highly addictive anti-depressants as an example of this. They cannot even begin to deal with the original problem (often a depression fully warranted by the circumstances in their lives) until they have dealt with this added, debilitating dependency on the drugs and the side-effects experienced as a result of those drugs.

The Dark Goddess is often portrayed as a horror; pictures of the Indian Goddess Kali show her tongue dripping blood and a necklace of skulls hanging around her neck. Or the Fates, from Greek myth, are seen frighteningly as spinning, measuring and cutting the life thread of each mortal. Celtic stories include the Washer at the Ford, an old woman who may be seen by a warrior on the eve of battle. If he sees her washing his own clothes it is a premonition of his death. The Dark Goddess deals in change, and death is one of those changes. We are perhaps overly aware of the death-aspect of change; whether it be leaving a job, ending a relationship or letting go of a treasured belief. It's hard for most of us, untutored as we are in the practices of the Dark Goddess, to do more than accept change as inevitable; only rarely do we welcome it joyously. And actual, bodily death, of ourselves or our loved ones is the great dread of our culture. Because of this the Dark Goddess is customarily shunned.

But this is only half the story of the Dark Goddess. Her other face is the face of compassion. No-one would deny that death itself can be compassion; the release of suffering, the clearing away of the old to make room for the new, the gentle embrace of completion. But because we are so afraid of this aspect of the Dark Goddess, and so avoid it, we are not familiar enough with her compassionate side. When we hear the Dark Goddess calling us we tend towards terror in whatever expression most suits us; avoidance, denial or outright refusal. Yet these events, of meeting the Dark Goddess and experiencing what begins as loss and questioning, are the same experiences that fuel the amazing leaps and developments we make once we are out the other side, revitalizing our lives. When the Dark Goddess shows up, things are going to change; and this contains both good and bad; longed-for and also dreaded events. Becoming more accustomed to change lessens our fear and inability to deal with it, as well as opening our eyes and hearts to the essential patterns of change.

There have been times I had no warning of the Dark Goddess' advent in my life. Meeting her then was like being in the path of a tidal wave or a cyclone. Other times I heard the warning clearly. I prepared myself to meet her on one front, when actually she was coming from somewhere else. I got it wrong, and went down struggling. Other times I heard right, jumped right, met her halfway and went with relative grace. Still, I find meeting the Dark Goddess excruciating, simply because it means confronting what I have been avoiding and have a lot invested in keeping hidden. Meeting the truth of my soul again is like purging bitter drugs out of my system; cleansing and freeing and agonizing and desperate.

Some of the things the Dark Goddess has to say we may have suspected for a long time. When she tells us to work less, play more, rediscover our creative and spiritual selves – well, we've known that forever. But nothing she offers comes without a price. Will you put off buying a home, to follow that voice? Will you downgrade your lifestyle, your address, or your career ambitions to follow it? Will you risk disapproval, invite questions and judgments from family, workmates, friends? Or will you do what we all mostly do, fold that voice away inside, tell it *not yet* or cover it up with the refrain of *I can't think about that right now*?

The Dark Goddess waits at the heart of the Underworld. She may guide your journey in, she may be the voice you hear calling to you, she may hold the answer you seek. But when you meet her she will skewer you with her rapier eyes which see only the truth. She will flay you with the cries of her heart that have been ignored and she will hang you up to rot with her anguish that is your own. To rise again you must encompass patience, compassion, understanding and courage. All of these are attributes of the Dark Goddess and you will have as much time as you need to gather them. You must demonstrate these attributes not just towards the Dark Goddess, but towards yourself as well. Otherwise you will not be free to leave her realm.

Mapping the Underworld

This would all be terrifying if there wasn't some kind of a map, a 'how to' with directions so clear you really can't get it wrong. It's still hard, don't mistake that, hard and necessary and sometimes we experience it as grim and devastating; but it's possible.

There is a map. It's been passed down in the Greek myths; stories of Persephone's Descent and return, Orpheus' journey to rescue his beloved and Psyche's attempt to win Aphrodite's favor. This map also exists in immaculate precision in the Egyptian tomb writings and their elaborate instructions for each hour as one passes through the realm of the dead. More emotively, but with little specific detail, it is written into the Bible as the myth of Jesus' death and resurrection. You can even watch it, every month, as the moon gradually turns to dark, by increments, vanishes and then reappears, born anew but different; or every year at the Winter Solstice as the days shorten progressively until – a miracle – they turn around and begin lengthening again.

There is another story that tells not just the events, but the actual step-by-step of how to do it. It is the Sumerian story of the Goddess Inanna's Descent to the Underworld and her eventual return. Inanna's story; her voice, actions and responses sound familiar to us, understandable and immediate. This is a powerful and moving story that was saved from the endless editing and rewriting some other stories have suffered from by the clay tablets that record it being buried in the desert until mid-last century. This means that – translated – we get the myth the Sumerians recorded, four thousand years ago. This myth has been used as a model for women's psychological development by a number of writers, most famously in Sylvia Brinton Parera's *Descent to the Goddess*.

In all of these myths a protagonist makes a deliberate Descent and transition through the Underworld. Descents, Underworld journeys and meetings with the Dark Goddess can be deliberately entered into not just in myth or story, but by ourselves, and that is the main focus of this book. I believe all of us have – at least once, but probably many times through our life – experienced these things without having consciously chosen to undergo them, without understanding them clearly and without a map. I believe this is terrain we have traveled since we were children or teenagers. Not only does our culture have very little understanding or tolerance of this; but because we don't understand the necessity of such journeys and their place in the balance of our lives, we spend a great deal of energy postponing, avoiding and denying them. This avoidance, denial and postponement may be not only pointless but also regressive. In the end we go down, and any energy we have used to resist seems to add to the force with which we are propelled and held there.

Sometimes we have spent years down there in the Underworld, hardly knowing how we got there and certainly not knowing how to get out. We might have begun the Descent, perhaps not of our conscious choosing and then become stuck, half-way. Maybe we missed a crucial step in the proceedings and are unable to complete our journey. This can result in the feeling of living a 'half-life', just waiting for real life to resume, or even in giving up and resigning ourselves to a shadow-like existence. We may hardly recognize ourselves in the actual life we are living. These are symptoms of an Underworld journey that is incomplete. When we study the maps and practice walking these paths deliberately, the manifestations of sickness, depression, and alienation are far less severe, and we make discoveries that are hard to make when we are in the grip of real-life trauma. Walking into the Underworld willingly we have much freer access to the deep personal transformation which is an essential part of this journey; the renewal of the soul.

It is a young woman who ventures to the Dark Goddess in the myths, throwing out all our preconceptions that it should be a crone, or at least a wise woman who travels these paths. Persephone and Psyche are both young and even naïve; Inanna, although already a Queen, is robust with youth. To read this symbolically, we should not wait for wisdom in order to make our Descents. Should not, or can not. The youth of these protagonists shows that when we enter the Underworld we are starting from the basis of not-knowing, and compared with the Dark Goddess, the part of us that makes the journey is young indeed.

There are a number of related fields to this journeying to the Dark Goddess, including shamanistic soul retrieval and shadow work. During soul retrieval parts of the soul that have become lost or separated are retrieved by a shaman from the Underworld, and reclaimed for the one who lost them. Another approach, in the field of personal development, is known as shadow work. Shadow work addresses areas of darkness in an individual's life, behavior or personality (or sometimes those of a whole culture). These can be repressed traits, prejudices, areas of denial, addiction and self-limitation.

Shadow work and soul retrieval, while valuable in themselves, do not address the fundamental imbalance we carry between dark and light. In both the dark is largely cast as 'bad' (or undesirable), and both seek to bring everything into the light, to 'enlighten'. Shadow work in particular is not about according darkness half of the playing field. My reading is that shadow work is actually part of the light half of life – the daylight side. It deals with 'dark' issues in the light. In true darkness, after all, no shadows are to be seen; so fundamentally shadow work can only occur in the light. As part of the integration between light and dark this is perfect, because it is in the brightest, most empowered and most glorious places that issues such as fear, loss, death and letting go are highlighted. *The deepest shadow is cast by the strongest light* is not just a metaphor; it is literal truth. In darkness, contrastingly, we look for birth, transformation, and new beginnings.

Shadow work can function as an overture towards actual darkness; for its promises of personal empowerment and recognizing the true self are deeply related to the Dark Goddess. Approaching the Dark Goddess, however, involves a surrender on the deepest levels. This is a mythic, archetypal and initiatory journey; the specific results of which cannot be known or often even imagined beforehand. Dark Goddess work, and Underworld journeys, belong in the actual dark where there are no shadows and everything is merged. That is, until a light is struck; and that light is the light of dawn, of the birth or rebirth of the soul.

INANNA'S PREPARATION FOR DESCENT TO THE UNDERWORLD

Queen of all Heaven and Earth, Inanna (who in Babylon was known as Ishtar) was a young and powerful Goddess in the Sumerian mythos. The culture that birthed this Goddess, Mesopotamia, is called the cradle of civilization. It lay at the meeting place of two great rivers, the Tigris and the Euphrates. This fertile crescent of the ancient world gave birth to agriculture, writing, astronomy and early civilization. There was a vast temple system that oversaw land management, justice, sacred rites and civil celebrations. Over all this presided the Gods, and at one particular time the Queen of all the Gods was Inanna. We know her stories from the clay tablets inscribed four thousand years ago and discovered, pieced together and translated only during the last century.

The Inanna of these stories has defied and defeated Gods

much older than herself through a combination of wit, daring
and courage to assume great powers, that were not originally
hers. She is brave and beautiful, mistress of both the battlefield
and the bedroom; presiding over temples and courts. The love
poetry between Inanna and her consort Dumuzi is famous for its
sensual, evocative explicitness. Their love-making is celebrated
throughout the country as that which literally brings the animals
to bear their young and the fields to ripen. Inanna is adored by
all. She is the morning and evening star that we call Venus and
she shares many attributes with that Goddess. She is used to
getting what she wants.

The story of her encounter with the Dark Goddess is nearly
complete in its preservation and can easily be read in its transla-
tions and interpretations. *Inanna Queen of Heaven and Earth: Her
Stories and Hymns from Sumer* by Diane Wolkstein and Samuel
Noah Kramer is accessible and beautifully translated.

Inanna gives several reasons for her journey into the
Underworld; most enigmatically, that she hears it calling her.
Another reason she gives is that she is going to take part in the
funeral rites of her sister's husband, the great Bull of Heaven.
The third possible reason for her visit is that this trip is another
journey for the covert accumulation of her powers. Previously
she has visited and tricked a number of Gods elder to, and more
powerful than herself; assuming their powers when she
succeeds. She never mentions it, but it is possible that the Queen
of Heaven and Earth has the domain of the Underworld in her
sights.

Inanna has to go to the Underworld. For the story to work,
she has to go. To reunite with her sister and to bring together
what has been split apart – the light and dark halves of the
Sumerian Goddess – she must venture down there. For the Dark
Goddess does not leave the Underworld, and as she holds the
powers of both birth and death, she has no need to. It is others
who must journey to her realm.

Inanna knows that travelers to the Underworld do not return, and although she seems to believe she will be exempt from this, she does make provisions for rescue, just in case. She assigns Ninshubur, her loyal retainer, to wait outside the First Gate that leads into the Underworld. If Inanna does not return in three days and three nights, Ninshubur is to go for help. She is told to visit certain temples in a certain order and to appeal directly to the Gods there. Inanna is sure they will not let her remain forever in the Underworld.

Inanna also prepares for her journey by arraying herself in seven garments of power and radiance. It has been pointed out before that this is not usually the way one arrives at a funeral. These garments and objects are not just symbols of her power, they are the actual powers themselves. Thus her measuring rod and line – made of lapis lazuli – doesn't just *show* she is the one who measures out the fields and decides in the courts on matters of justice, it literally *is* the object that has those powers. Her possession of it grants her those powers. Thus its loss would mean her loss of those powers.

So Inanna sets off into the Underworld, much against the perceived wisdom and any understanding of how the universe works. After all, she is the Goddess of Heaven and Earth, most specifically *not* the Underworld, and since she has a history of visiting other Gods in order to wrest their powers away from them, or trick them into surrendering those powers, you might think her arrival would be looked upon dubiously. And I always worried that several of the Gods she so blithely entrusted her rescue to were the same Gods she had stolen powers from, previously. The Queen of Heaven and Earth is, undeniably, arrogant.

Imagining Inanna

I heard it calling me. The Underworld. Well, I heard a faint voice; I thought it came from there. From under my feet. From my sister, dark Ereshkigal. All alone down in the Underworld. Mourning, surely, the death of her husband.

I decided then. To visit her. To pay a call. A difficult place, the Underworld; no-one I knew had ever gone there and returned. But I, as the Queen of Heaven and Earth, surely I could travel there and return. She would not refuse me.

I gathered up my regalia. She would meet me in all my glory. I placed the crown of the steppes upon my brow, it conferred my Queenship. About my throat I placed the precious lapis beads, and also the double strand of beads that fell to my breast. I bound about me my breastplate, famous on the battlefield and also in the bedroom. I have welcomed men onto my spear and also into my arms. I wore the gold armband high on my arm and in my hand I carried my lapis measuring rod and line; that which was the power of measuring out the land. About my body I placed the robe of royalty.

I took with me my most loyal Ninshubur. She I set to watch at the First Gate. If I do not return in three days and three nights, I told her; You must go for help. This she willingly agreed to. I told her which temples to travel to, which Gods to appeal to. Surely they would not leave me, Inanna, Queen of Heaven and Earth, their precious jewel to rot in the ground. I had every faith I would return, one way or another.

I rapped on the First Gate. There was a long wait, a lot of scuttling around and then, slowly, the First Gate opened for me. I, Inanna, Queen of all Sumer, approached the Underworld.

The Sumerian stories, and pivotally the Gilgamesh myth, are a marker of the advent of patriarchy, the point in Middle East culture where control and power passed out of the hands of the temples into those of the king. Gilgamesh, history's first recorded king, according to these stories refused to join in sacred marriage with the Goddess; Inanna. Traditionally the king's source of power would have been this very thing – his alliance with the temples, as symbolized by the yearly rite of the sacred marriage – and his refusing it (yet remaining king and indeed engendering a line of kings) surely denotes the ending of the old system of the distribution of power in the city-states. Perhaps Inanna's venture into the Underworld is part of her battle with Gilgamesh; if she were victorious down there, and able to combine the powers of the Underworld with her own powers, maybe she would stand a chance.

In a little circular unfolding of events Inanna was so furious at Gilgamesh's rejection of her (or Gilgamesh's effective challenge to and over-throwing of the temples) that she caused the Bull of Heaven to be released, to battle Gilgamesh and show the extent of her wrath. As history, or myth, will have it, Gilgamesh and his comrade Enkidu killed the Bull; an almost unimaginable act. This can be aligned, astrologically, with the precession of the equinoxes and the passing of the bull sign (Taurus) into that of the ram (Aries) which occurred at about this time. This Bull of Heaven, Gugulana, was the husband of Inanna's sister, Ereshkigal. It is his funeral rites Inanna experiences a sudden need to go and witness, down in the Underworld. No wonder her sister was a little mad at her.

MY OWN INANNA STORY: PREPARING

I did my first deliberate Descent to the Underworld more than twenty years ago. Twenty women committed to a nine day ritual Descent, held during a Women's Spirit Camp in a freezing springtime and led by the indomitable Robin La Trobe. Robin had read Inanna's story in Wolkstein and Kramer, had read Brinton Parera and was convinced she was reading an ancient women's initiation map.

That Descent was one of the turning points of my life and is still seared into my mind. At the end of it I made a conscious choice, knowing it would change my life forever when I became a Priestess of the Goddess, a choice that had never occurred to me before that moment. But unexpected as it was, in that moment of making the decision I felt I'd been courting it for years, perhaps my whole life. That was after my meeting with the Dark Goddess.

I had arrived at the Women's Spirit Camp by listening to some faint voice, calling to me from within. I was a resolute feminist, sturdily ignoring women who searched for a return to women-focused spirituality. In the feminist-activist circles I moved in the women's movement was split into two camps; political and spiritual. We worked together on the same protests, gatherings and conferences, but those on the spiritual side did fluffy bits round the edges and those on the political side retained a faint contempt for activities based on feelings and rituals. We were the hard core.

As well as this I was a writer. I wrote mainly short stories and I noticed, over one particular year, the metaphor of the Goddess creeping into my writing. It appeared in three stories in a row, always in a different semblance, for a different reason; but still. I did not want to be repetitive so I decided the next story I wrote must not include that theme. And I couldn't do it. The writing called out for it, yearned for it. The story needed the Goddess in there. I gave in; but I felt I had to get to the bottom of this. I had to work out what the Goddess meant to me, since apparently she was more than a convenient metaphor.

I started attending women's spiritual events. I found them lightweight; frustrating in their simplicity with no power, roots, or deep rationale. I had startling moments, none-the-less, when I went deep into my own psyche in a way unfamiliar to me except in dreams, but then returned weeping with exasperation at the inability of these events to frame that depth.

I went looking for something strong. I said to myself, *I need something really powerful*. Deep and with conviction. I was imagining something almost tangible, another life I could step into sideways for a course of lessons and then return, satisfied; my questions answered and my knowledge increased. Not long after I had determined this I visited an occult bookshop in the city. When I got to the counter to pay for my book the young man serving looked at me and said, *I've got something for you. Wait a minute. They only came in this morning,* and dashed away out the back of the shop. I had never met him before.

When he returned he gave me a paper flyer. *This is for you,* he said; *I know you'll want to go to this.* I held in my hand an advertisement for a Women's Spirit Camp. During its nine days, a Descent of Inanna would occur. When I got home I put the piece of paper on my desk. It called to me, challenged me and I'd always loved myths. The idea of exploring one so tangibly had its own magic. Nine days with no escape, with a group of women I didn't know. It promised power, depth. I signed up.

PREPARATION FOR DESCENTS IN OTHER MYTHS

Persephone and Psyche are two other Goddesses whose stories include a Descent to the Underworld. Their myths have been subject to any number of re-writings, forgettings and imaginings during the years between when the ancient Greeks recorded them and us reading them now. They remain, however, vivid and popular in their retellings and as with Inanna's Descent many commentators, analysts and novelists have been inspired by their stories.

Changes to a myth can be made for cultural reasons – to render a myth more understandable to a certain audience (children, for example, or those of a different culture or time) – or more politic reasons; such as to turn what may originally have been a myth empowering to women into one that teaches women a very different lesson. There are also cases of genuine misinterpretation, either through language difficulties or cultural differences. Perhaps all of this has occurred to these particular myths, but I think it's not hard to get back to something approaching the original (or fundamental) story behind our current, commonly recognized, stories of Persephone and Psyche.

Often what changes in successive versions of myths (or fairy stories, or possibly even the stories we tell of our own lives) is not so much the events that occur, as the interpretation of those events. It is the motivations, emotions and the implied consequences of certain behaviors that are subject to such interpretation and reinterpretation, thus inadvertently – or purposefully – changing the listener's understanding of the myth. When we simply look at the events of the myth, *devoid* of the meaning assigned to them, quite logical (but previously hidden or ignored) alternate meanings present themselves, explaining events and characters' actions quite differently. At the very least the stories become open; the events can be viewed free of any judgments of narration. Since myths encase sacred mysteries I believe they were always and fundamentally about a multiplicity of meanings, open to interpretation. Some of these meanings are paradoxical; that is different interpretations can co-exist, and both Persephone and Psyche's stories abound in such paradoxes.

Persephone

Persephone is the only daughter of the Greek Grain Goddess, Demeter. At this early stage of her story she does not have a name, being known as Kore, a word meaning *maiden*. She is not strongly differentiated from her mother and sometimes Kore is depicted simply as a younger version of Demeter. Demeter's realms are the orchards and fields of cultivated land and she is occupied with the increase of life; the production of corn and grain, the birthing of lambs and the flowering and fruiting of trees. Wherever she goes her daughter is with her.

I imagine a baby Kore, cuddled to her mother's breast, wanting nothing more. I imagine Kore as a small child, playing in the meadows with flowers and lambs, knowing nothing else. When I think of her growing up I imagine her playing in streams and wondering where they go, wanting to follow them. I imagine her lingering at the edges of the woods, wanting to know what's in there. I imagine her climbing trees to spy out different places;

29

maybe cities or deserts or the sea. But Demeter does not go to those places, and Kore is always with Demeter.

Kore grows up. Demeter does not have a partner, a consort. Why would she think that Kore might have one? Demeter is happy in her endless summer; why would Kore want anything different? Is this not a very common mother-and-daughter story? Demeter is endlessly busy; would she notice that Kore is not quite so involved in what is, after all, Demeter's work? Would she notice, other than distractedly, if Kore began drifting towards the edges of things like a teenager does, maybe twisting her hair round her fingers while she yearned and dreamed for something different? Could Demeter conceive that an entire repudiation of her way of life is about to come, or would she just think, *that girl will grow out of it*? What did our mothers think and what do we, as mothers, think of our daughters?

Because what happens, the event that occurs, is that one day the earth opens up and Kore disappears into the Underworld. In the story there is a flower – and I imagine it growing at the edge of the cultivated places, on the edge of the wild – that the maiden had never seen before and when she went over (to pick it, to smell it, to be seduced by it) a gaping hole opened in the earth and the passage to the Underworld was revealed. She vanished into it and by the time she returned she had eaten the pomegranate seeds and become Persephone. The whole thing reads like a metaphor for the sexual act.

Current versions have it that Hades, Lord of the Underworld had his eye on Kore for a wife. Since he knew Demeter would never agree, he created the flower to attract the young maiden and then abducted her (possibly with a chariot and six snorting black horses). Feminist re-writes suggest that maybe she just went looking for her own life, and the flower is a symbol for a world beyond her mother's world. But maybe she was drawn to a demon lover; a God brimming with seductive sexuality who promised to take her away from her mother and change her life forever. I think the flower symbolizes her own just discovered sexuality and that she went willing. But whatever occurred, she vanished. And someone heard it happen; the Goddess Hecate, the crone Goddess who guards the crossroads of choices, and of life and death. She was the only witness to the Descent of the young Goddess.

Psyche

Psyche's story begins unfortunately. Too pretty for mortal comprehension, she is compared to the Goddess Aphrodite. Although Psyche's two sisters marry, no-one will approach her father for Psyche's hand; her other-worldly beauty is too much for them. Meanwhile Aphrodite becomes furious as her own temples are neglected by those who worship beauty, in favor of this mortal girl. She arranges for Psyche to be removed; telling Psyche's parents to prepare her for marriage to a fearful monster and then chain her to the top of a mountain. In awe of the Goddess of Love and Beauty, the parents do as they have been instructed.

Aphrodite then sends her own son, Eros (also known by his Roman name, Cupid) with his bow and arrows to ensure the ending of Psyche. But seeing her while she sleeps Eros is awed by her beauty. He manages to prick himself with one of his own arrows (and it's hard to imagine this is anything more than a story told to his mother, afterwards) thus falling in love with the maiden. He's in a bit of a bind now, caught between mother and beloved, so he calls upon the west wind to waft Psyche down into a secluded mountain valley, where he has a palace with invisible servants who will provide for her every need. Surely it is more than co-incidence that the west wind was the very same wind that blew Aphrodite ashore, when she was born from the sea? This double appearance of the west wind indicates more than a passing relationship between Psyche and Aphrodite; and has echoes of Demeter and Kore's relationship; that of the older/younger versions of one Goddess.

Once Psyche is in his palace Eros visits her at night, secretly and without revealing who he is. They are lovers but he tells her that if she ever sees his face, he will come to her no longer. So the thing is begun, the great love story of Psyche (the soul) and Eros (love). The soul is in love with love; and love (which is the God) is in love with the soul, the soul of a mortal. And it takes place in darkness.

There are many interpretations of this darkened courting of Eros and Psyche (their very names translate as Love and Soul). Is he (Love) after all, the fearful monster she was promised to and her vision of him would cement that meaning? It has been cited as the darkness of ignorance (as in *love is blind*). There is also the inference that a mortal is not allowed to see the Gods clearly but can only experience them in the dark places; hidden as the truth of them is hidden. But I suspect it has a more essential meaning, which is that the moment of impregnation, sperm into ovum – to be followed by the cell dividing and new life – happens in the darkness of the body. The moment of a seed casing cracking open to send down a root happens in the dark earth. And in this darkened time of loving, Psyche does become pregnant to her lover.

Events progress. Psyche asks to see her sisters and – with misgivings – Eros allows the visit. Her sisters plant doubts in her mind; saying that since Psyche has never seen her lover undoubtedly he is a demon or monster. They implore Psyche to take a lantern while he is sleeping one night and gaze upon his face and Psyche eventually does this. When she gazes upon Eros she recognizes him for the God he is and – simultaneously – one drop of burning oil from the lamp falls onto his skin and wakens him. As he has always threatened to do under these circumstances, he leaves.

Why exactly does he leave? Why was it so important Psyche never saw his face? Why would Aphrodite (who has remained in ignorance of Psyche's whereabouts and her son's activities until now) be any the wiser? Perhaps the myth has simply come to a new stage of itself; we are out of the darkness and new choices must be made. The drop of burning oil is one of realization; Psyche has realized who her lover is and Eros has realized he can conceal himself no longer.

Once Psyche understands Eros is not returning, she sets out to find him. She goes to many temples, and beseeches help from many Gods and Goddesses. All tell her the same thing; that the only one who can help her is Aphrodite. Eventually, reluctantly, Psyche goes to Aphrodite's temple and makes suitable offerings and prostrations.

Aphrodite sets Psyche four tasks. In the versions I've read she seems determined Psyche will not succeed at these tasks, but that's an interpretation. Her actions are to set the tasks. None of these tasks – and Psyche succeeds at the first three – are things it is possible for a mortal human to accomplish. Yet Psyche – with help, advice and support from various non-human quarters – accomplishes them. With the help of some ants she separates a pile of mixed seeds into their component parts; with the advice and help of the plants growing nearby she gathers a bag of fleece from the ferocious golden rams and with the help of an eagle (sometimes thought to be Zeus himself) she obtains a goblet of water from the river Lethe, or the Styx. Perhaps her success is giving us a clue that she is special beyond merely her beauty; and even, perhaps, that Aphrodite is playing a role greater than that of jealous Goddess. Aphrodite's demands of Psyche force her to face challenges, make alliances and grow up. It could be seen that she is preparing Psyche for something.

The fourth task Aphrodite assigns Psyche is to venture into the Underworld and retrieve a box of beauty ointment from Persephone, the Dark Goddess. Psyche – who throughout the entire story has regularly given way to fits of despair – takes herself up a high tower and prepares to dash herself to the ground. It's almost the exact opposite of what she's been asked to do. She's told to go into the Underworld and instead she climbs a high tower. Perhaps this is similar to what we ourselves do, when we feel forced to enter the Underworld; we attempt to get as far away as possible.

The tower speaks to Psyche, as do the reeds growing down the bottom of the tower. The tower and the reeds have links to both heaven and the Underworld, by virtue of their vertical structure, planted in the ground but reaching upwards. Between them, they tell Psyche where to find the entrance to the Underworld and what to take with her. She is to take two coins for the ferryman, one for the crossing in each direction and two pieces of bread for the three-headed guard dog, one for the way in and one for the way out. She is told to stay focused on her task and ignore all distractions, even if these are pleas for help. Importantly, she is also instructed not to open the box of beauty ointment, once she receives it.

PREPARING YOURSELF FOR DESCENT

The Underworld has been called by many different names and covers many different experiences. Perhaps you have experienced enormous helplessness at some time in your life, due to illness; poverty; abuse; depression or another factor. Perhaps you have experienced the results of severe trauma, such as prolonged shock; severe injury; post-traumatic stress syndrome; a near-death experience or the sudden death of a loved one. Perhaps you have experienced the loss of a future in the death of a child or a relationship; a career failure or a debilitating illness or condition. Perhaps you have suffered a form of anomie; feeling dislocated from everything around you due to medication, a mental illness, 'reme stress or cultural dislocation. All of these things, and 'ther versions of them I would call Underworld experi-

'acterized by feelings of loss, feeling captive

34

within the unknown and needing release. Almost always, release is set in motion (eventually) by some understanding or change that takes place within ourselves. External things also begin to change; but usually as a result of the internal changes we have made. Afterwards we can look back and see how this happened. From that point we rebuild our lives, and it seems they become fuller, deeper and richer in that rebuilding than they were prior to the Underworld experience. I believe that is because we have met the Dark Goddess while we were down there, and integrated some of her truths into our lives.

You might think it is bad enough when these things occur by themselves without having to seek them out, to venture into the Underworld deliberately. But it is precisely when we learn to venture into the Underworld willingly we learn the most, integrate the most deeply and – extraordinarily – remain conscious enough to create a map that will mean next time we plummet down without warning, we will know what to do. I also believe these experiences become, not exactly less severe, but less debilitating; we retain more perspective, detachment and understanding as we repeat them, and as we learn to travel these paths more consciously.

In their myths Inanna, Persephone and Psyche are all preparing for a visit to the Underworld. Inanna's intent is clearly stated; she will go to the Underworld to visit her sister, Ereshkigal. She has prepared a back-up rescue and arrayed herself in her finest powers. Persephone is clearly seeking something *other*, without knowing what that is (and who among us has never been in that situation?) She has been prepared only by being born into the caste of Goddess and by her close alliance with her mother, the powerful Demeter. Psyche is a mortal following the directives of a Goddess in order to achieve her heart's desire. She has received assistance from many allies and they have told her how to successfully enter and leave the Underworld.

All three of them heard the Underworld or the Dark Goddess calling to them. Inanna has heard her sister calling. Persephone has heard – maybe the appeals of Hades, maybe the cries of dead souls, waiting to be reborn, or maybe just the 'voice' of a single flower, different to all other flowers. Psyche has heard Aphrodite, issuing demands. All of these calls urge them to make the perilous journey. What happens to them on the way down, and in the Underworld itself, will be different for each, but all their stories will have similar resonances. Each of the three will meet her nemesis. Each one will die, and be reborn to a more integrated whole. Each will bring changes with her, that on her return will ripple outwards; and each will carry within herself a continued bridge between the Underworld and the upper world, the dark and light.

What does it take us, mortal women with busy, demanding or uncontrollable lives to prepare for a Descent? A long holiday? Desperation? A dedicated spiritual practice? In a way preparing is beside the point, as the very nature of the Underworld means that everything you've previously learnt is more or less useless – you are always on new ground, always giving birth to the unknown; but preparing does assist with your state of mind, as you go down. Firstly, and at the very least, it takes awareness to prepare; Inanna's listening to a whisper, coming from the earth; Psyche's finally seeking out Aphrodite's temple; Persephone's notice of a flower she had never seen before.

Something calls. Something jostles at the edges of our awareness for attention. Something unquiet is stirring, something unusual, even unique – that has never been a factor before. In some way the life we take for granted is disrupted and there is a schism; an opportunity to descend. Sometimes, if we do not choose to take this opportunity – do not recognize it, do not dare, do not risk it – it goes away, of itself. For a while. But mostly – after getting louder and more obvious, sometimes over many years – it trips us up and down we go, unwilling and unprepared.

It's fair to say this is how most of us discover the Underworld.

There are advantages to keeping an ear out, to anticipating its concerns and going willing, once called. These advantages might be summed up as speed, grace and self-determination. They do not, essentially, change the place we arrive at or the work we have to do when we get there (and before we can leave), but there is tremendous empowerment in self-determination. Once we have settled on our own course (even a difficult or dangerous one, such as a journey into the Underworld) we feel much more in charge, positive and determined.

When we go unwilling we are always half looking over our shoulder, trying to head backwards at the same time as we are inexorably being dragged forwards (downwards). It's faster if you know where you're going and start off there yourself, rather than resisting and perhaps visiting many blind alleys, holding stations and blank zones along the way. Things are also faster when we have decided in advance to go gracefully, rather than having to battle our disbelief and unwillingness at every turn.

Inanna and Psyche went down willingly, although Psyche had been contemplating suicide as an alternative; a pertinent choice, because in entering the Underworld at all, some part of us has to die. Inanna had all the choices in the world, being Queen of Heaven and Earth but for some strange reason (not understandable by anyone else in her story) she settled on this one, thus provoking her utter disempowerment in the one realm she could have no influence in. Other stories of Underworld visits, where the protagonist returns to the upper world include those of Orpheus (also Greek and seeking his dead love, Eurydice) and Jesus Christ (who visited the realm of death by dying in his mortal body). In these stories also, the protagonist went willingly. This is why I believe that Persephone also went willingly; the great pattern of these stories is to go willing.

What does it take, to prepare for a Descent?

Pack light, for everything will have to go before the end.

I have dreamt all my adult life of a sudden pressing emergency. In the dream I have moments, only, to gather what I will take with me. Often I have my son with me, always young in these dreams, and I must pack for us both. Sometimes I have to carry him. In the dream I am in my real house of the current time. I have a day pack, or something similar and what I take are things like a change of underwear, several pairs of socks, an extra jumper, our raincoats. I have time to put my boots on. I choose which boots to wear and I choose the most practical. In the dream I walk past my beautiful books, my jewelry, my mementos and not only do I not pick any of those things up, I feel inside me a tremendous distance from them; a relief almost, in leaving them behind. I grab a blanket as I leave the house – not my favorite one, simply the closest. And then I am gone, carrying the pack on my back and my child on my hip. I have practically nothing with me and yet it is everything. Apart from my son, not a single thing I am taking with me am I emotionally attached to.

I have dreamt this hundreds of times; perhaps thousands. It is an emergency – it is life and death – and yet in it I am freed.

The allure of this freedom is one of the beckoning promises of the Dark Goddess.

RITUAL: PLACING YOUR EAR TO THE GROUND
The intention of this ritual is to help you recognize the call of the Underworld.

Time: 1 hour. Spend half your time on the first part of this process and the remaining time on the second part.
You will need:
- Pen and paper; preferably a journal
- Colored pens/pastels – optional
- A cushion or pillow (and optional shawl or blanket)

Part 1: Your Past Times in the Underworld

You can do this ritual in front of your Altar, or at a special or sacred place.

- It's nice to light a candle or incense, or otherwise acknowledge the beginning of your process.

I suggest casting a circle, or moving into sacred or ritual space at the start of Part 2 of this ritual but you may choose to do it now, at the very beginning. If you are not certain how to cast a circle there are many books and websites that offer different suggestions. Basically casting a circle is a way of demarcating the time and physical area where you will do your ritual. It is an action or series of actions that proclaim – to yourself and the spirits/Goddess/energies – that within that time and space you are dedicated to the sacred, to your ritual. Casting a circle acts as a reminder to yourself to stay within the ritual. It is also an energetic container for whatever you do, and a focusing technique. If you form the habit of casting circles or creating sacred space this practice will allow you to alter your mindset more quickly and easily from the 'mundane' world into the sacred world. (Or to transition from the upper world into the Underworld.)

- When you are ready to begin, draw four columns on your paper, either across the width of two pages, or by turning an A4 page on its side. Give the columns the headings *The Underworld*; *Timing*; *Issues*; and *Changes*.
- In *The Underworld* column list the occasions in your life you have had a lengthy time (probably months but it may be years) when you did not feel in charge of your life; when you were floundering, lost, out of control, adrift, stuck or profoundly blank. These times would have been accompanied by a sense of knowing something was

wrong, without necessarily knowing what was wrong. They may well have been accompanied by your denial, your protestations that everything was fine, or by a genuine lack of understanding that anything could be different.

- You may only have one or two instances, or you may have many.
- In the next column, *Timing*, record your approximate age at the time of each instance you listed in the first column, and how long you think – or guess – you spent 'in the Underworld' on each of those occasions.
- In the *Issues* column, record the main issues or reasons you now – with hindsight – believe caused you to spend time in the Underworld on each of these occasions.
- In the *Changes* column, record what you learnt, put into practice or changed in your life or yourself, as a result of each visit to the Underworld. You may have to sit with this for some time, thinking back and reflecting. Changes that appear to have little connection with your Underworld experience may actually have occurred very shortly after-wards… Most probably, these events are related.

Now look for any patterns in what you have written. For example, you might notice that every five years you have an Underworld event, even though they are all about different issues. Or you might notice the issues are the same ones, repeating again and again, though each time the results are different. You may notice the time you spend in the Underworld is getting shorter – or longer. Look for your unique patterns. Record these patterns on the following page; these will be important later on, when you begin to make your own map of the Underworld.

Part 2: Listening to the Underworld

Now put your writing away and spend a few moments preparing yourself to journey within. Read all the instructions through fully before you begin. It does not matter if you remember every one of the suggestions or not; the main thing is to concentrate yourself into the listening. Some or all of these suggestions may come back to you once you begin the process, or your ritual may take its own path. This is a ritual you can repeat, even many times, so do not worry about getting it perfect this first time. Your intent and the actual listening you do will be enough.

- If you did not cast a circle or create sacred space at the beginning of the process, do so now. (There is a description of how to do this on page 107). Some alternative suggestions to casting a circle are burning incense or smudging the room; using a breathing exercise or a brief, clearing meditation.
- Lie down on the floor (if you prefer, you can do this outside and lie on the earth). Place your ear to the ground (or the floor). Spend fifteen minutes or so listening intently.

Listen for the sounds that come from the earth. You might hear rumbling vibrations of traffic or building noise, you might hear the sea or the wind. Listen more deeply, imagining you can hear water running underground; rocks and earth shifting around; the roots of living things growing and processing nutrients; insects moving around in their earthy homes and tunnels.

Listen more deeply. You might hear the heartbeat of the earth, or its breathing. Listen for your own heartbeat and your own breathing. Listen to how these interact with the earth.

Listen deeper. Listen to the molten core of the earth. Listen to its tides, its seasons unfolding. Listen to life stirring and listen to decay and decomposition.

Listen more deeply. Listen to your own inner voice, to your sister-self who lives in the darkness. Listen to the cries of your soul. Listen to any faint whispers.

- After fifteen minutes, sit up and record what you heard; in words or in shapes, colors and pictures.

You can repeat the second part of this ritual whenever you like; for example when something is wrong in your life, or if you realize you have been forgetting to listen to yourself. You could use it periodically; literally in the dark of each moon, during your period or at any other time you feel is appropriate.

It may take many times practicing this before you can easily hear your inner voice, or feel confident that what you hear is not just 'made up'. A useful method is to make sure you record whatever it was you heard or felt and then check back a month or so later. By then it will usually make painful sense, even if it didn't at the time.

Even if you feel you are not able to hear anything useful, listening is still worthwhile. It may take a long time for your inner voice to trust that you really will listen to it, or for you to learn to hear it. Allowing some time to listen is a basic step in learning the maps of the Underworld, and in the preparation for journeying to the Dark Goddess.

MOVING INTO THE SACRED REALM

Moving into the sacred realm is an essential part of preparing yourself to visit the Underworld. One way to think about making a ritual sacred, or moving into the sacred realm is to imagine you are working with three layers.

Firstly there's the outer layer; which is composed of the actions you take. What matters here is what you actually, physically *do*. It might include making altars, offerings or dedications;

dancing or going out into nature. It might include cleansing in the form of a ritual bath, a fast or a time of meditation and prayer. It is the form of the ritual and functions as a container for the other aspects of ritual. When this outer layer exists on its own, it is sometimes called an *empty ritual*.

Then there's a second layer. This consists of what is happening within you, and it is encouraged and supported by what's happening in the outer layer. Being willing, being true, carrying out not just the actions but the *intent* of your ritual or journey make up this second layer. You may find it helpful to whisper a mantra under your breath, to focus on an image or to chant or drum for a while to take you further inwards. When these first two layers are in concert, the ritual will feel satisfying and alive.

There is yet a further layer. This is the mystical one, and may be different every time. It is the moment when the ritual takes off, when you slip across from one realm into another, into the sacred; into the realm of the Dark Goddess herself. In this layer you will feel the divine all around you and within you, and you will sense yourself as being in an altered, perhaps luminous space. This does not happen every time you do a ritual, no matter how well you are managing the other two layers. It is enough to work with the first two layers and invite this third one to manifest. A ritual will still be meaningful without entering the third layer; though it may be more memorable and feel more powerful when you do slip across the boundary into this realm.

To Make Sacred

To sacrifice something is to make it sacred. In making an offering to the divine – whether it is an object, our energy or purpose or an activity – it becomes sacred. It's as if that act of giving something over to the Gods renders it part of their realm, and therefore sacred. This is worth knowing because, famously, on the way down into the Underworld sacrifices are called for.

When we understand that we are not just losing something in a sacrifice, but *giving* something, and in fact gifting it to the divine, sacrificing important things begins to make more sense.

Inanna sacrifices her seven regalia of power – those very things that make her the Queen of Heaven and Earth. Persephone sacrifices all she has ever known – her relationship with her mother; her life as Kore, maiden of the fields and flowers; as well as the whole of the upper, daylit world. Psyche has been a sacrifice herself; to a jealous Goddess. Later she sacrifices her relationship with her hidden lover, and later still she makes further sacrifices, when she has to refuse help to those weak or dying, who ask her for the precious resources she cannot afford to give away if she is to fulfill her quest in the Underworld. Each of these Goddesses must sacrifice everything to their purpose – and it is a sacrifice that *makes sacred*. Because of these sacrifices, they are able to continue. Without them, they would not make it into the Underworld.

These sacrifices turn Inanna into an ordinary being who can die just like anyone else; they leave Persephone stripped of her past role and Psyche strengthened to her purpose. This turns out to be exactly what each of them needs, in order to undergo the transformation of the Underworld. So their sacrifices actually cause them to be available for the transformation of the Underworld. In making these sacrifices, they have made themselves – and their journeys – sacred.

How do we get ourselves into this place, where we are *made sacred* or where we enter into the sacred?

The experience of entering the sacred for me has been like a gate opening, a potential opened up where I hadn't seen one before. Each time I have to chose to step through it. I have never felt I could afford to hesitate, standing there – there is enough time for an intake of breath – but it may well be different for others. In stepping through the gate I sacrifice everything that was my previous life, because I have moved somewhere new.

Recognizing the gate is relatively easy. I become aware this step forward exists, a choice of a new action and if I take it everything will change irrevocably. It is as tangible to me as a physical doorway. It usually feels as if it is straight ahead of me, occasionally slightly to one side. It has never been an effort to step forward, in fact usually it has been a shining light, a lifting of burdens, a great relief and a deep sense of rightness. I also have not felt any judgment attached to stepping through it or not. Simply there was a choice and within a breath, the choice was made; not really by my mind for no thinking was involved, no calculation, so perhaps it was a choice made by my spirit. Sometimes the gates are smaller ones, significant in their own right but not with the grandeur of life-changing choices. They may reset an understanding, correct a direction that has gone slightly awry, or reconnect one with one's own life-force or soul purpose.

As for summoning the gate – I don't know how to do that. I know how to make space for it to arise. For me the way towards the gate is in deliberate, focused ritual, usually sustained over several days. This might involve small sacrifices of time, attention and priorities. It is not supposed to be impossible, but it should lift you out of the ordinary. Sometimes I pursue this when things have gone seriously wrong – a relationship failed, a misdirection taken – and sometimes it is simply a lack of inspiration or direction that pushes me out the door and towards such change.

There's a labyrinth about thirty minutes drive away from my home. One time I was an emotional mess and a friend said to me, *Do something radical*. I decided to walk the labyrinth every day for a week. To fit it into my ordinary life I had to do it at all different times; early morning, the middle of the day, late afternoon. I took my son with me, and another child as well, when I was minding her. I walked the labyrinth in the rain, and one day as a storm was brewing, under lightning and thunder. On the first day I made up a mantra as I entered the labyrinth; *Each step I take is sacred. With each step I move towards my dreams and the fulfillment of my soul.*

I repeated the words under my breath, walking to the rhythm of them. Each day I noted which word I was speaking when I came to the centre of the labyrinth, and which word I was speaking as I exited. Those words were never insignificant. On the first day I arrived in the centre of the labyrinth on the word *sacred.* My final step to exit the labyrinth, on the way out, was on the word *dreams.* So on that first day I remembered that my dreams were sacred.

On the second day *each step I take* was what I was saying both as I entered the centre of the labyrinth and as I exited. So I was shown that each and every step counted on the path towards my sacred dreams. I felt these steps referred to the literal, physical steps I was taking as I moved around the labyrinth.

On the third day it was the word *fulfillment* both on reaching the centre and on leaving the labyrinth and on that day, the mantra turned itself into a song. As I was repeating the words they gathered a tune to themselves which built and reinforced as I continued. So it seemed to be singing to me that walking the labyrinth was fulfillment in itself; that by doing this I was living my sacred dreams.

On the fourth day it was the words *each step,* emphasizing again and again that each, every step was important. On day five I stepped into the centre as I sang *each step* and my final step out of the labyrinth was on the word *soul.* Each step is a part of my soul.

Days six and seven were a kind of ecstasy, where I felt the entire song and labyrinth to be an extension of myself; the song vibrating through me, my steps shimmering through the labyrinth in a sacred ritual weaving of the dreams of my soul. I felt *made sacred* by these seven sequential trips into and out of the labyrinth.

Another time I wanted to *make sacred* I went on ten consecutive days to sacred sites, some of them many hours drive away. This was made more difficult by the fact it was over Christmas and New Year. On about the third day everything began to fall into place; how to get to these places started fitting in with everything else I needed to do, and what I was doing once I got there became simple, clear and sequential. In the end it was no effort at all to carry out this ritual, though when I'd first contemplated it, it seemed somewhat mad and I doubted I would find the energy or will to do it. Another time I spent a weekend enacting, by myself, one of my own workshops as rigorously as if I was teaching it to others.

Almost always when I have begun these processes I have not known how I would be able to complete them. There were practical problems of time and logistics as well as my doubt of my own commitment or ability to carry through. I also doubted the meaning and worth of such actions. Each time I have been stunned into awareness very early on in the process, where it seems like this action or series of actions is the pivot of my life, and I would no more stop them part-way than I would lie down and die. Further, as they unfolded I received a depth of meaning and a joy in the process that had been missing in my life.

Being Willing

The first layer of making sacred is the form; what it looks like, what the actions are. This is constructed, maybe altered as you go along; but it is simple enough. It involves, for example, walking a labyrinth every day for seven days; or following your meditation practice or taking art classes. It involves sacrifice in terms of making choices and priorities. The second layer is within the self. Sometimes I have constructed such rituals for others, at their request. That is, I have presented them with a form I believed would take them deeply enough inward that they would have opportunity to enter the second layer.

Once, with a friend, I constructed an elaborate ritual for another woman. She had asked us for a ritual to help change her life. We wrote a three-part ritual that spanned a whole night. A major theme of the ritual was letting go of control, and so we told her that we would choose the day and when we came for her, she must come with us. We set up the entire ritual for a night we knew she had nothing on, and we rang her in the afternoon to tell her it was that night. She said no. She was not willing. She did not enter the first layer.

Another example was when my partner of the time asked me for a ritual to free him from a defiance he had flung up against the Goddess. He had begun to realize her breadth and knew he had made a mistake. He wanted to retract. I dreamt of a ritual for him. In the morning I told him to go and find the fallen branch of a gum tree and he had dreamt that same night of a fallen branch, so he did it. Then we went to an ancient site of power and initiation and camped there. At dusk I made offerings of honey and water to the spirits of that land; I asked for their permission to work this ritual and I felt to them it was like leaves blowing over the ground, they barely noticed it.

Before dawn the next morning we went into a circle I cast. I called upon the Goddess to witness that this man had spoken unwisely, rashly and he wished to retract his challenge. I asked her to let him go and I said he would offer a price to do so; a sacrifice. And then I stood back.

He followed the form of the ritual. He lashed himself with the branch of twigs and leaves and yet he did not enter the second layer. He did not sweat, or bleed or weep. He did not become the ritual, he did not make himself sacred in it. He did not change, and so become able to twist his fate and open a doorway for himself. When he finished I closed and grounded the circle. We packed up and went home. I had seen he was not willing to enter the second layer, and so the third layer had no chance to arise.

The father of my child asked me for a ritual as he was turning forty. I asked if he wanted it to be life-changing, or just a celebration and he said, *Life-changing.* I told him to invite those he loved, both men and women, and for him to arrive an hour beforehand. On his arrival, I handed him a set of written instructions.

The instructions were to have a shower and then, taking only a sarong, to walk to the tipi that stood in a field not far away, where he would pass the final hour of his life. In the tipi were water and a pen and paper.

He turned from me and went. I heard the shower running. I caught a glimpse of him as he walked away from the house, towards the field. There was someone watching him, though he did not know it. He went to the tipi and entered it. The watcher remained – as a safety measure, to catch hold of him should he choose not to do the ritual, to ground and re-orient him – but that was not needed.

After an hour all the men he had invited, plus our twelve year old son, entered the tipi. The man in front had a blanket with him, he threw it over the father of my son and said, *You are dead. Lie down now,* and he did lie down. Had he struggled, they would have held him down.

For nearly an hour they conducted a memorial service. Each of them spoke in turn of the man who was now dead; what they had valued in him as a human being, what their relationship had been to him and how they might miss him, now that he was no longer in their lives. My son led a song that they all sang. From under the blanket, in the centre of their circle, he heard all this. I believe it came to him through the second layer.

Then one of them blindfolded him and led him to the house, saying that this was the passage into the Underworld. Unresisting, he came into the circle of women. We did not speak, though we sang and murmured as we laid him down on cushions. We massaged him with oils and gentle touches, then

we waved perfumes under his nose; we fed him bites of straw-
berry and dark chocolate and gave him sips of water. We stood
him up and danced with him, blindfolded amongst eight or so
women and finally we took off his blindfold and told him he was
reborn.

The men came in and we made a circle and sang together, men
and women with him in the middle and he laughed and wept and
could not speak and eventually sang with us and then joined the
circle and we danced, all together and wildly, with life. I don't
know for sure, but I believe at some point he had entered the
third layer. His willingness made the way for him.

So I have said there are three layers to such a ritual. The first is
the form, the second is entering within the form. The third is
spirit – God or Goddess, Great Spirit – it is when that reaches out
and touches you. By then you are nearly one with it, anyway, so
perhaps it is you reaching out to touch yourself; but you merge.
The tiny part of you that is always alive with spirit, as spirit,
becomes all of you and all of you is within that. This can be a
moment, a second, or much longer. Usually it feels like
suspended time, however long it actually lasts.

The first two layers of this ritual are relatively under your
control – you can construct them, you can enter into them deliberately, or at least with practice. Many spiritual traditions are
built around forcing the third level, also, to occur at your will, but
for myself, my practice is an ecstatic one, so I invite and do not
compel it. It comes on the breeze, on a breath, in a heartbeat and
to me it is stronger that way. I believe, and experience, this force
as immanent and everywhere. I create conditions to allow myself
to attune to it – and then, sometimes – often, when I have sought
it, and many times when I have not especially sought it – it is
there. And I am one with it.

The Sideways Descent (not recommended)

I could feel it mounting; a dark wave threatening at the edges of my awareness. The Dark Goddess. I was in England and due to come back to Australia, while my partner stayed behind for a few months. It had been a while since I did a Descent, but not so long that I had forgotten what it was like. I thought I'd get in fast, meet her half-way and head off the whole process. In theory, this is not a bad idea. In practice... it took an unexpected left turn.

I looked hard at my life, through critical eyes and saw two major weaknesses, from my own ethical standpoint. I was incredibly relieved that neither of them was to do with my relationship, which I valued beyond measure.

I went back to Australia determined to deal with those two issues. I remember being incredibly grateful that my relationship was so secure and I could rely on it, while I worked on other parts of my life. I felt strong enough to tackle anything while I was within the safety net of that relationship. I pulled those two issues apart, piece by piece. I did rituals, process work and deep inner questioning and I found new understandings and resolution. I challenged myself, dug deep and rewrote the parts of my life I thought had been questionable – not without some difficulty, but I felt proud of taking the initiative, of being proactive. I changed my behavior. Things around those two issues began to change, in response.

Then my partner came back from overseas and my relationship fell apart. It was an utter surprise to me. I was not prepared for it. I was devastated. I went to the deepest, darkest place I had been for a long time, alleviated only – not by the personal work I had just been nobly undertaking, in completely different areas of my life – but by my knowledge that the path DOES come out the other side, if you keep moving. Darker it got; darker and darker. I did remember, from earlier times, to keep going. One of my friends said that watching me terrified her, she only wanted me to come back. Many people advised me to forget it, forget him and get on with it, but I was in the teeth of the Dark Goddess and – agonizingly – it had to be done her way.

It was a Descent with all the stops pulled out, and even though I'd seen it coming, felt it coming – heard it, if you like, heard her calling out to me – still I'd got it wrong and so I went down, sideways it felt like. It was like jumping and misjudging the landing, or the monster appearing in my blind spot. Probably reading that you can tell my mistake; to think I knew what I was doing, to try to write the Dark Goddess' agenda for her. Not that the work I did was wasted, or wrong; it was useful in its own way. But obviously I wasn't listening to her. I was listening to how I wanted it to be. My offerings, such as they were, were about controlling my life, not about honoring the Dark Goddess.

Dream

I had a dream that I shivered, huddled naked with a dozen other women. We were on one side of a dark volcano of swallowing flame. It was impassable and yet it was the only way. It was very dark, impossible to see anything much, but I had a sense of the vast, lost unknown on the other side. There was confusion, uncertainty. We were stuck, unable to go backwards and unwilling to go forwards.

A vast magnificence of woman-shaped darkness stepped past me, to begin the passage through. She was shadow and energy, mutable but unquestionable and I stood up, and stepped so fast it was a blur until I was within her shape and now we were together, darkness enormous, blazing with light. I turned my head to look back at the women as I strode forward and called out, *I am the Dark Goddess, follow me* – and my voice boomed and resounded off invisible walls. My immensity and my footsteps created the way forward. My naked body flared light out in all directions; I was fierce and clear and no longer remotely myself and my walking carved a passage, literally through the darkness.

I did not know if they followed or not; I could not think of it.

And I was in ecstasy, physical, emotional and spiritual ecstasy. Every atom of me was vibrating with joy, life, awareness and power. I had a moment of wonder, knowing I was the Dark Goddess but still I was blazing with light; I was the only thing of light in that place of utter darkness and I was radiating it; it came from me, not reflecting off me but originating in me.

RITUAL: HONORING THE DARK GODDESS

The intention of this ritual to make further preparations to journey into the Underworld, by honoring the Dark Goddess and creating a back-up plan for yourself.

Time: 1 – 1.5 hours; this can be split into two parts of roughly equal length

You will need:

- Pen and paper; preferably a journal
- Materials for creating an altar or offering (details below)

Part 1: Honoring the Dark Goddess

Does it make any difference to give an offering to the Dark Goddess, whether before, during or after a Descent? At the very least it makes a difference to you, to your awareness and sensibility and the manner of your approach. This is part of *making sacred*. But I believe it also makes a difference to her.

Read through these suggestions, then choose what you will do. It's good to choose something slightly challenging; such as creating an altar if you've never made one before. If, on the other hand, you make altars all the time, you may choose to write a song, make a painting or create a spontaneous dance as your offering to honor the Dark Goddess. Encouraging yourself to step outside what you are comfortable with is good practice for descending into the Underworld.

- Choose how you will signify you have entered sacred

space. You could light the candle on your altar; say a prayer; cast a circle or spend a few moments in quiet meditation.

- *One option* for this ritual is to create an altar dedicated to the Dark Goddess, or make over an altar you already have, dedicating it to her. An altar can be as simple as a small table or shelf on which is placed a piece of fabric and on that, some representation of the Dark Goddess (a picture, small statuette, a seedpod or anything else you feel is appropriate) and a candle. It also can be much more elaborate. When you light the candle, or when you spend time at your altar – meditating, doing the processes in this book or just sitting – you are offering your time and attention to her. This is honoring the Dark Goddess.

- *Another option* is to make a gift for the Dark Goddess. One time I made a mask, half dark and half light to represent how she gives birth in the darkness. Another time I drew a purple and red glitter spiral on a teardrop shape of black cardboard and wrote a poem in gold that wound into the spiral, letting her know I was heading towards her. I have also made offerings of jewelry; precious mementos that I felt tied me to the past and other things. You could make an offering of food, of art or of music.

- After you have made your gift you can place it on your altar; or put it in a dark box or bury it in the earth. If later you wish to dispose of an offering it should be burned or buried. If it is bio-degradable, you can leave it outside on the ground. Often I have buried offerings under a beautiful tree.

Part 2: Organizing Your Back-Up

There is one more thing to consider before you set off into the Underworld. Inanna organized an elaborate back-up plan for her rescue, in case she needed it (and she did). Persephone was observed by Hecate (who later assisted Demeter in her quest for Persephone's release), and Psyche had a divine lover, who proved he had what it took when things were most dire. Even though you are planning to consciously set off to meet the Dark Goddess, you are also planning to return; and the myths show the return scenario works better when there's been some forethought and some outside help is available.

What is your back-up plan? How do you plan to rescue yourself? Who is your Ninshubur, your Hecate, your Eros?

Friends can play these parts for us, as well as counselors and support groups and priestesses. You might choose to do a Descent in a group, working ritually together following a particular myth; or each doing your own personal work, but in conjunction with the others. Of course we can also leave parts of ourselves symbolically 'on guard' outside the gates of the Underworld, and it's useful to acknowledge and name these parts before we set off. Particularly if you are already in crisis or difficulty, or you think some very tough issues await you, it's best to have more than one of these back-up systems set in place. Three is ideal. They could be a counselor you are seeing; a support group you are part of and a wise friend. Or maybe your magical group; your own sensible, grounded aspect and your High Priestess. Or your partner; your own self-discipline and your best friend.

- On a new page in your journal, or on a fresh piece of paper, write down your back-up plan. This will be unique for every person; it should be tailored to yourself. Make sure you are creating a system you know you will work for you, rather than one you think looks 'right' or seems to follow my suggestions. You don't have to rush this; if you can't complete it in one session, come back to it later. You might also like to check in with the people you've put on your plan.

- Your back-up plan should cover points such as: Choosing one person or group on your list that you commit to checking in with every week while you are doing this work; including a clause involving warning signs (such as drinking, taking medication that you wouldn't normally take, any sign of not being able to eat, sleep or exercise); and steps you will take if you feel yourself really getting lost, beyond or outside the plan outlined in this book.
- One thing I have found useful and done many times is write a letter to myself, before I set out on an Underworld journey. If you'd like to do this, begin with your name at the top and write down all the reasons why you should, eventually, return from the Underworld. Sign your own name, with love. Save this piece of paper – on your altar or in your journal – for a time when you might need encouragement or a reminder of why you need to continue your journey, and not get stuck part-way.

MAKING A MAP OF THE JOURNEY

One of the most valuable things you can do during a conscious Underworld journey is make a map. This means that not only are you keeping track of the terrain you're coming through (a sort of retrospective map), but also you will have a map for the next time you choose to venture into the Underworld. Your maps can also be helpful to others. Just imagine if you could go to the computer and search *Underworld Maps* and get a couple of dozen really descriptive, detailed commentaries of other women's Descents. Your mapping of your journey is pioneer work. I've made maps in journals, with mandalas and in stories, and this book is another version of my map.

I recommend that you map each of four stages of this journey; the Preparation for Descent, Descending to the Underworld, In the Underworld and Coming Up from the Underworld. These are the four parts this book is divided into, and at the end of each of them I'll remind you about making your map. Maybe you will share these progressive maps, as you make them, with someone who is part of your back-up plan, so they know how you are progressing.

Journaling is one popular way to make a map and it's accessible to everyone. You don't have to write poetically, or neatly, you just have to record events and emotions. You can do it in point form, if you like. Or in poetry. Another way to record your journey is using art – again, you don't have to be an artist – you can make mandalas, patterns of shape and color or drawings or abstracts of your feelings and experiences. If you are musical you may choose to write songs about your journey to the Dark Goddess, or instrumental compositions; if you are a dancer you may choose to choreograph a piece. What I am trying to say is – record it. Don't just create a one-off retelling of your experience, (spoken, danced or in some easily destructible form, like a sand sculpture); make it permanent. The best maps are those you can go back to when you need them, and that may be years later.

You can choose just one method of map-making and follow that through for all four parts of the journey. Or you can experiment with different forms; such as a poem for the first part, a painting for the second part... choosing whichever form seems to you to frame that experience the best. A map does not have to be perfect or infallible but it is at least a record of where you went and any wonders you discovered. It can also be a record of very practical things such as how long something took; what you felt like before and after particular events or moments; rituals you did and inspiration or support you picked up from other people, books or spiritual practices.

This book can be a guide, a kind of general map but parallel to that, you will also be creating your own, personal map. You will be mapping as maps are actually made; backwards, recording where you have come from with all the territory ahead of you an unknown blank. It's understandable why ancient maps have dragons or sea-serpents in the places that haven't been traveled yet. The unknown, blank areas are much more frightening than those known coastlines, mountain ranges or currents; enough to imagine sea-serpents might live there. But where you've already been can tell you a lot about where you're going, as well as simply recording your progress to date. Your own personal map will have a vitality and immediacy for your own life that this book, my map, can only support.

Map Making

Choose a medium that appeals to you and create a map of what you have been through so far, in your preparation to enter the Underworld and visit the Dark Goddess. Following are some different suggestions, but feel free to branch out and find your own form of expression.

If you are working through this book part by part, it's good to make a map of this first stage, before you move on. That way you can crystallize information, sensations and understandings of this part before they get reinterpreted by later events and insights. Even if you want to move onto the next part straight away, at least jotting down some notes or sketches for your map will help you to recall exactly how you felt when you come back to them.

Journals

I like journals. I usually have three going at any one time. I have a daily diary, where I write exactly one page every day. What I think of as my journal and workbook is an A4 notebook and in this I keep notes, ideas and plans of rituals and meetings, and rough drafts of articles or submissions. From the other end of the book I've used it as a process book – which I write in only as I need – for emotional processing, recording dreams that didn't make it into my diary or outpourings of local anguish. I usually have a third journal going – for any specific process I'm involved in, such as the eleven months I recently spent exploring the Kabbalistic Tree of Life.

I like journals with unlined pages, good quality paper and nice covers (sometimes I cover them myself, with fabric or wrapping paper). I prefer blank pages so I can be creative – draw diagrams, go sideways on the page or literally put drawings in amongst the writing. I like it that my writing is sometimes big, sometimes small, sometimes slants up the page. But choose whatever you like; a tiny A6 notebook if you want to carry it everywhere, a huge sketching pad or a school exercise book. You could keep a journal on your computer.

But try to use one. Much of the Underworld stuff you will deal with is truly subterranean – it requires excavation and, like dreams – it can go right back to where you got it from if it's not pinned down somehow. You might like to talk to someone else, as one way of pulling this material into the upper world, once you discover it. But many people don't like to do this, or not right away; or they might have no-one they feel they can share it with. Or they might have a support group or a therapist or best friend they see once a week – but sometimes much more happens in a week than can be covered in that one meeting.

You can write poetry in your journal. You can draw pictures in it – whether or not you are any sort of an artist. Sometimes feelings are easier to express in color and shape than words, especially when you're trying to describe emotions, visions or dreams that have no words to them yet. You can copy quotes or exercises from other books into it. You can write in point form. You can write flow-of-consciousness. You can debate the pros and cons of something. You can make lists. You can keep a record of where you've been and write a travelogue of how things look and later you can read it like a map; to help you understand your journey through the Underworld.

Art

You may be an artist or someone who hasn't picked up anything more colorful than a biro since you were a child. You may paint in oils or create crazy appliqué or sculpt or mosaic. Art of any kind is a powerful medium for expressing emotional and spiritual experiences – experiences that can be very difficult or unsatisfactory to express in words. I have found when I record my dreams in a drawing, rather than in writing, they leap off the page at me and I see far more in them than I do with the ones I've faithfully put into words. After all, they didn't come to me as words on a page, and sometimes art can be much more loyal to the experience, as well as elucidating aspects of it in quite a different way than words do.

Some ways to use art in making your maps would be:

- Creating four separate pieces of art, one for each stage of the journey, all in the same medium. Four mandalas, for instance, or four charcoal drawings.
- Creating one piece of art with four distinct sections expressing the four stages; whether this be in embroidery, glass mosaic or pastels.
- Creating four distinct pieces of art for the four stages of the journey; such as a sculpture, a watercolor, a short video and a ceremonial robe.

Music, Dance, Poetry, Short Stories

Again, you can create four separate pieces of music or one piece, with four movements. You can use instruments you are familiar with, or those you have little or no experience with. You can write songs, or one song with four verses. The same goes for dance, poetry or short stories; or any other format you can think of that you want to make maps with.

PART TWO:

DESCENDING INTO THE UNDERWORLD

DESCENDING INTO THE UNDERWORLD

The Dark Goddess doesn't live in the upper world, on the surface of things; she's in the inner. You might get flashes – or whispers – of her while you're up above, living your ordinary life but you won't get to meet her, not really, until you've descended. This descending is the journey we make towards her.

Most times we visit the Underworld we're not willing. This creates a few extra problems; slowness, confusion and resistance. Of the four parts of the Descent story, the actual Descent into the Underworld is the part we find most difficult. Preparing; well, anyone can put a brave face on that. And once you're there, of course, there's nothing to be done. And coming up afterwards more or less makes sense. But – descending! Fighting that off seems like the good fight; noble, even, to resist being dragged into the mud, being abducted, seduced, tricked into an impossible bargain. The things we have to do on the way down into the Underworld are for each of us, uniquely and in every situation, the hardest things. *Do not go gently...* And we don't. And usually it's not gentle.

On the way into the Underworld we have to give up control. We have to let go of things that are dear to us, positions we've worked for; order and behaviors we rely on; relationships and objects so precious we hardly know how to continue existing without them. For each woman (and maybe each time it will be different) this includes our children, our creativity, success, health, security, marriage... the list is endless. These are the things that tie us to the upper world. It's all very well to understand that life will continue if we suddenly die – that's beyond our control and we manage not to think of it too often – but to know that life will continue without us if we just step out of it for a while... that seems even more painful to contemplate than actual dying.

Our resistance to letting go of those things dear to us is so monumental we can spend years on a Descent. On the stairs, as it were, between one state and another. No longer entirely in the upper world, but not reaching the Dark Goddess either. Lost in the labyrinthine paths of the Underworld that always bring you back to exactly where you were, until you surrender. In this state we may cling even more strongly to those things that are left to us, not understanding – and never having been taught – that this is to delay the whole, inevitable purpose. If we were to have the power to cling to being awake, and so never sleep; how would that be? If we had the power to hold summer here forever; what would happen then? If individuals did not die; how could that work? So, too, attempting to remain forever in the upper world is not sustainable. Delay on the way to the Underworld does not change the pattern, it merely delays it. And the consequences of delay – like delaying sleep or winter or death – may have their own cost.

Descent is a death-like process but it is not death. On the contrary; it is life. Stripped of everything we will meet ourselves again, our soul. From that point on we can rise, like spring returning, to renew our lives with fresh meaning, vigor and insight. But the way down is hard. Perhaps because our culture has put so much emphasis on *things* – on owning objects, on achieving success, and on personality – to let go of all of these (or even any of these) seems truly dire to us. Maybe Buddhists, or the world's poor, or those who maintain voluntary poverty and a life of service would not have such a hard time. Almost the only way I have found to do it successfully is not to get too caught up in the idea of what is being left behind.

There's a process I use in workshops where each woman is asked; *Will you give up your (job, beauty, personality, relationship, children…)?* Each woman is asked this question many times, with a different thing to give up being asked of her each time. I tell them the only answer they can give is *yes*. Or they can stay silent.

And if they stay silent, unable to say *yes*? The question will be asked again. The same question will be asked as many times as it takes until they can answer *yes*. To find a way to speak that word *yes* one may have to imagine one's own death, where we will no longer have a choice. One may have to go on faith alone, knowing that the myths of the Goddess carve a path forward into the darkness and trusting that this path emerges again, eventually.

There's no bargaining with the Underworld. There's no bargaining, either, with the states of life and death we've been born into, so you'd think we'd be used to it. We cannot hang onto the way things are *now* and expect them also to change. We cannot hang onto the very things we are needing to change. We cannot visit the Dark Goddess, or meet our soul again while we are still clinging to the form of things, to the vestiges of the upper world. We are born naked, with nothing. This is how we will emerge, again, from the Underworld. It is not unlike the idea of a soul choosing to incarnate and having to leave behind all knowledge and memory of other states or previous lives.

Once the excess is gone – and when we're talking about the Underworld, nearly everything is excess, including possessions, relationships, habits, personality, activities, status and just about anything else that isn't pure *being* – there's bliss. Oneness. Meditators discipline themselves to reach this inner state. Cultists try to merge with it. Artists pursue its vision doggedly. Athletes force themselves into it. We all have moments of this oneness; in love, in nature, in music, in deep ritual, in dreams. If you think about the times you have experienced such simple being, such oneness, you are close to imagining what it is like in the Underworld; a place where extraneous things have been left far behind and the utter essence of existence is concentrated and almost exploding within you.

There are different paths you can take to reach the Underworld and the Dark Goddess. I like to think of the journey as a series of gates (or stages); because Inanna's story has gates, and that is the model laid down so strongly in my imagination and almost my body. Following the Greek myths, or Egyptian, or Christian, one would find a different model of Descent, but I believe that process would result in a similar outcome.

It can seem to happen in a flash – suddenly finding ourselves at the bottom of the Underworld, staring at the Dark Goddess and remembering, then, a whole train of events and precursors that probably you could name as gates, now; now that you are already through them. This has happened to me a couple of times. I remember pinning everything on a single phone call to a friend, who I had imagined might save me from a dire, complex situation. In the few seconds it took to process her dismissive response to my carefully concealed plea for help, I seemed to tumble down the entire way. Or it can happen with agonizing slowness, dredging down one gate at a time, through months or even years until we wonder if this process ever has an end.

We have forgotten the rules. The rules are to surrender; to say *yes* and to keep going. This actually applies to a lot of things, not just Descents. Learning meditation, for instance; as well as many other spiritual disciplines and some psychological and self-help processes. Arguing with the process doesn't help; although we are so good at arguing, at rationalization, at postponement, obscurification and distraction. If we think of a Descent as a labor, laboring to give birth to ourselves, perhaps we can go a little easier with the tide. After all we accept that fighting, instead of surrendering to the process of labor makes birth more difficult; even potentially more dangerous. We accept that birth has only one direction. One cannot stop the process (or only very briefly) and there is no way to finish it but to go through it, one way or another. And it's best when the laboring woman works with the labor, with her body, with the baby trying to be born. Not that it won't happen if she doesn't; but it is much easier on her when she lends her will, strength and direction to it.

It may be useful to look at areas of your life where you have deliberately said *yes* to a process, even though it may have been uncomfortable in the short term. This does not only apply to giving birth, it may have been a medical procedure (such as treatment for cancer); the practice of a spiritual discipline; a self-imposed program of exercise, learning or creating (art, music, or building a house); or the experience of raising children.

Following the Wheel of the Year taught me to keep saying *yes*. The Wheel of the Year is the pattern of solstices, equinoxes and cross-quarters (two of which are commonly known as Halloween and May Day). These eight festivals are spaced throughout the year and mark seasonal changes. For many thousands of years and across many continents humans have linked their times of celebration and observance to these festivals. Like the moon's cycle this sun cycle is a pattern with a birth (the Winter Solstice, when the sun is reborn each year); a growing season (through the cross-quarter of Imbolc and the Spring Equinox); a period of heightened fullness (May Day or Beltaine and the Summer Solstice); a time of decline but also harvest (Lammas, or Lughnassa and the Fall or Autumn Equinox) and a fallow period (Halloween, also known as Samhain and through to the Winter Solstice again).

These eight festivals can also be placed around a compass or circle, giving eight directions, each linked to one of these seasonal festivals. For about ten years I actively assigned myself to one, after another, after another of the eight directions, spending a month working with each one of them. At the beginning I had huge resistance to ever entering or staying in the direction of Lammas. I looked forward to reaching the Autumn Equinox. I welcomed the Winter Solstice. Sometimes I feared the uncertainty of Beltaine. But going round and round this wheel for years, gradually these preferences left me. As I experienced each position over and over again, I felt more and more deeply that each one of them is a crucial part of the whole, and that each one reflects all the others. I had intellectually known this before; I just hadn't experienced it so vividly. I went beyond personal preference. I learnt to say *yes* to each section, each movement and each change and to experience the beauty of that movement, that *yes* which occurred regardless of which direction I was moving into. And in doing this I learnt how to hold the whole of the Wheel.

When we say *yes* to life, we get to live. Yes to being born, to childhood, adolescence, to our twenties and all our choices we made, one by one; yes, yes, yes.

This saying *yes* to life is not the same as saying yes to any form of abuse – mental, physical, emotional – and should not be confused with it. We are saying yes to the processes of our own life, and though for many of us this may involve accepting what has happened to us in the past, it does not involve condoning it or continuing to remain in situations which are dangerous or where we are abused. On the contrary, these *yeses* are reclaiming our most essential selves and they are the full-hearted, empowered *yes* of reclaiming our soul. They do not involve compromising ourselves, just letting go of attachment. As a very basic guideline, when someone else asks for your *yes* in a situation that is good for them, but not for you, your *yes* is not required and may be harmful to your ability to say any genuine *yes* to life. It is one of the more sinister aspects of abuse that those situations can be among the hardest to let go of our attachment to.

We can practice saying *yes* by looking at what has already happened in our lives. Saying yes to our past – simply agreeing that it has occurred, not that it was ideal or that we approve of it – sets down a formula for accepting things we might prefer to (uselessly) argue with. Once we understand how to accept *yes* and the detachment that comes with that; then in a Descent to the Underworld, when saying *yes* is obligatory, we will find ourselves more easily able to say *yes*. Yes, yes yes yes yes yes yes. Yes that happened, yes I accept it, yes I'm surrendering, yes I'm moving past it. This is the movement through the Underworld's gates, on the way down.

The Short Cut

There are two ways to get where you're going; the scenic route and the short cut.

We usually take the scenic route. On the scenic route we spend a lot of time trying to understand exactly why this is happening (whatever it is) or why it's happening to us. The scenic route can involve many detours; to painful areas of your childhood, relationships that didn't work out, and any number of personal issues that may call for your attention. The scenic route often involves stop-offs, where we entirely put aside the immediate issue and focus instead on something else; someone else's needs, for example, or trying to prove ourselves one way or another. Avoidance also features heavily on the scenic route; pretending (even to yourself) that nothing is wrong, or that things will get better by themselves (which they might, but avoiding them will not speed this on); or even flat out denial of the problem. Except, underneath, you know it's there. And underneath – sometimes – you catch glimpses of the short cut.

The short cut cuts to the chase. It doesn't bother with too much except getting where you want to go, faster. It's not concerned with all those subtle shades of feeling and meaning, all those little agonies, gentle setbacks and sympathetic asides. It's the core. For the hard-core. For those who know where they're going and want to get on with it. Cut the crap, forget the excuses and don't bother with the scenery. There's less struggle, with the short cut; and you stay in the present without detouring.

The scenic route is longer, sometimes infinitely long. There's lots of scenery; and by that I mean things to take your eye, distract you, things that absorb your attention and ask for under-standing. If my partner criticizes me, for example, which results in me feeling bad about myself, the scenic route might involve one or more of: trying to make myself feel better by going shopping; or to the gym; or receiving praise from someone else; or asking for reassurance from my partner; or remembering all the times previously in my life someone criticized me and understanding how it affected me; or doing inner-child or family-of-origin work; or making self-affirmations; or learning not to listen too deeply to what my partner says; or criticizing my partner in return; or agreeing with my partner and losing my self-esteem... It doesn't stop. The scenic route has a lot to look at. It doesn't solve the initial problem, though it can teach you all sorts of other things. Hopefully one of the things it teaches you, eventually, is that this is the scenic route and there also exists a short cut and the short cut is faster.

The short cut involves acknowledging your truth and also letting go of controlling the situation. In the example of being criticized by my partner and feeling bad about myself, the short cut looks something like saying at the time or very soon after, *I feel so hurt that you criticized me. I'm really trying my best.* Because I have declared myself (my truth), in effect I have let go of any effort to control or manipulate the situation. I have not concealed it (thus maintaining a belief that everything is fine); I have not used it to amp up an argument; or saved it for later ammunition. Techniques for this kind of short cut involve such things as: making 'I' statements instead of 'you' statements (*I feel furious you didn't finish the cleaning* instead of *You're hopeless at cleaning*); showing your partner how you feel; and asking what is underlying a statement or behavior. The short cut is short, to the point. It deals with the problem, directly. It can be almost impossible to spot the short cut, until we've been on the scenic route for a while. Even then it generally looks pretty unattractive, so often we take a few more loops on the scenic route. But the short cut's always there, when you really want it.

It's a little brutal. It's not polite. You won't end up understanding your deepest feelings and motivations. But it's fast and efficient. It's the scissors of the Dark Goddess, cutting through the knots of life. Mostly, we have to be pushed through unbelievable agony before we're willing to contemplate it. Then there's usually this dreadful sense of, *Oh I knew that all along, really*. We were just – putting it off.

Is that all? Wasn't all that soul searching worth anything? Didn't we gain a deeper understanding of ourselves and the situation; didn't we learn compassion and flexibility and other people's points of view? Well perhaps we did, but the motive was suspect. I think the motive was *delay* and *self-protection* and *willing blindness* and *reluctance to change* and so all that self-reflection could have been better employed, further down the track. Smoke and mirrors, that's what it was and in the end we came back to where we were at the beginning, still with the same thing to do.

A deliberate Descent, even a ritual one, is the ultimate short cut. There's no more hanging around trying to understand intricacies, or managing complex situations. No more waiting, hoping things will resolve themselves. In a Descent you are not worrying about the past, and you can't take it with you. In a Descent, at least in the short term, there's no future; or only a very narrow future of meeting the Dark Goddess. There's just the present, and that present is filled with acknowledgement of truth, and letting go. The short cut, in other words.

Of course sometimes it's not so easy to pick when we should be searching for a short cut (they are often hard for our eyes to pick out amongst the engrossing details of our scenic route) and when it's okay just to shrug and acknowledge, sometimes life is like this.

I have come to think it's worth taking the short cut whenever I possibly can. Maybe that's because I'm in a hurry, but maybe it's that sense of freedom, aliveness and simplicity I get when I dare to take it. It's worth it. Worth forgoing all that understanding, contemplation, self-examination and lengthy delay. Sometimes short cuts can be really obvious, and – obscurely – I've often found it easier to take them when they are huge and life changing, whereas the smaller ones can elude me. Initially I find it easy to buy into an emotional mire; but when I realize that emotional mire will take years to resolve, the short cut suddenly looks very attractive.

INANNA'S DESCENT TO THE UNDERWORLD

The Sumerian Underworld is reached by passing through seven gates. When the gatekeeper realizes who is waiting outside the First Gate he rushes away to consult with Ereshkigal, the Dark Goddess who is sometimes referred to as Inanna's sister. Ereshkigal thinks it is a great joke that Inanna is venturing into the Underworld. She counsels the gatekeeper to lock all the gates against her and at each gate to remove one item of her powers. The gatekeeper is obedient to this, opening only the First Gate for Inanna and, as she steps through it, removing the crown from her head.

Inanna is not expecting such indignities. *What is this?* she demands as she steps through. *Quiet, Inanna*, she is told. *The ways of the Underworld are perfect. They may not be questioned.* (Translation from Wolkstein and Kramer.)

She continues on. At the Second Gate her necklet of precious stones is removed; at the Third Gate her double strand of lapis beads is taken and at the Fourth Gate her breastplate. At each gate she asks, *What is this?* but we can imagine her voice becoming less strident, less certain as she loses power after power and as the way becomes deeper and ever darker. At every gate she is given the same answer; *Quiet, Inanna. The ways of the Underworld are perfect. They may not be questioned.* And so she proceeds, although clearly now the great Goddess of Heaven and Earth is not the one calling the shots and the journey has become immensely different than the one she embarked on.

At the Fifth Gate her gold arm-band is taken from her; at the

Sixth Gate it is the lapis measuring rod and line and at the Seventh Gate, finally, her robe which is called royal (and is literally what makes her royal, or even, perhaps, a Goddess) is taken. Without it hers is just an ordinary body. Naked and bowed low, she enters Ereshkigal's chamber, the heart of the Underworld.

Imagining Inanna

Seven gateways I went through; seven circles of hell I entered, into the deepest and the last.

At the First Gate it became dark and I could no longer see. Always I have been the queen of light, always I have ruled in sunlight or by starlight or with candles in the temples. There was no light, no light on the path to hell. Nothing I had experienced prepared me for the absence of sight. The darkness was such that I had to feel my way; I could not see the angles of the path or where it led, though my feet told me it went down.

At the Second Gate my voice seized up. I tried to talk to myself, to hold the fear at bay but the darkness pressed in on me as if it were a hand held to my mouth. Sometimes there seemed to be demons, leaping about me, but when I questioned them the words came out strangely and I no longer sounded like Inanna.

At the Third Gate I began to lose my breath. Panting I was, and yet going downhill, not up. As if the darkness reached still further in, inside my mouth to strangle me. I choked in terror, gasped for air. The air, when it came, tasted heavy, metallic and dank. I felt suffocated, as if I could not get enough of it. The Underworld invaded me.

At the Fourth Gate my hope left me in a great, trembling wave. I stumbled a moment and became aware that I walked along a narrow ledge. I pressed my body against the earthen, rocky wall; to the other side of me was nothing. Depth. I heard the demons' laughter about me and I feared that if I fell I would never recover the path. I tried to turn around and found I could not go back.

As I passed the Fifth Gate I became old. I felt my legs begin to shiver and creak. I thought I had been on that path a hundred years. My back ached, my hand on the wall trembled, my feet stumbled. Even my heart began to feel erratic in its beat. My fears increased; how much more likely that an old woman would fall from a steep, underground path than a young one? And yet I had to go on.

At the Sixth Gate all of my powers deserted me. My power of reason, my power of decision, my power of action. Nothing made sense to me any longer; why I was there, or why it was I should not let go and fall into the pit below me. I heard the demon voices loud and louder, but I could not understand what they said and I could not think what to reply. I no longer had any faith in myself, or that I would ever escape.

At the Seventh Gate I dropped into the void. I lost my body, I lost consciousness, I lost everything. Inanna was no more.

MY OWN INANNA STORY: DESCENDING

For my own Descent of Inanna it was unseasonably cold, a late spring. It rained, coldly. I was sleeping in a tent and the hall we had transformed into a temple was rustic and chilled. Around us the Australian bush dripped, its mists and grey-green colors dulling the exterior world as we plunged deeper and deeper into the mythos of Sumer, of the Goddess Inanna and her unseen counter-part, Ereshkigal. For each day of seven days, one day for each gate, we sat – mostly in silence – and created our own versions of Inanna's regalia. For the First Gate we made crowns. Mine was bracken and silver cardboard, with a crescent moon.

On the second day we made small bead necklaces; and on the third, a long double strand of beads, using dark blue beads that mimicked lapis lazuli. On the fourth day we made breast-plates; mine was yellow satin-covered cardboard, with tiny silver stars. On the fifth day we made arm-bracelets from twisted copper wire; I made a serpent that coiled around my upper arm, its head extending down towards my elbow. We made measuring rods and lines on the sixth day; I chose a tall green reed and trimmed it with narrow ribbons threaded with feathers, beads and silver stars glued to the ends. On the seventh day we made robes; mine was a caftan from heavy, blood-red fabric, with a silver star over my heart.

Each day we began with a temple invocation and a prayer to Inanna. One morning I was chosen to read the prayer. As I stood facing the altar with the book in my hands and began to speak, I felt a voice speak through me. The words shifted around in my mouth, the emphasis changed, the places where the pauses arrived were not chosen by me and I would have placed them elsewhere. I felt I was speaking through time – from an impossibly distant time – and that the words had a life in them, in this context, that was beyond me; beyond my powers of interpretation or imagination. I felt they were subtly altering me, refining me as I spoke them; that they retained a power that had not been diluted, merely laid aside for a few thousand years.

From the fourth day Ereshkigal was included in our prayer. As the days went by, she got louder and louder. We began to understand that Ereshkigal was the purpose of this whole journey, Ereshkigal was where we were headed and it was Ereshkigal's story we were discovering, as much as Inanna's. After five days we spoke a prayer to Ereshkigal and included Inanna. It became clear the whole Descent is in service to Ereshkigal. The myth is known as *The Descent of Inanna* but really it could, and perhaps should, be called *The Descent to Ereshkigal*. We learnt this as we invoked Inanna into our lives and our whole orientation became towards the dark one, Ereshkigal. We began as a temple of Inanna. We became a temple of Ereshkigal. After we had completed our journeys we took on the title of Priestesses of Inanna/Ereshkigal; and that Ereshkigal's name came second did not imply she had the secondary role, but the underlying one.

Each day after we'd made our sacred adornments we stood in meditation while one by one we descended through a symbolic gate. We crossed a line held between two women, one of whom removed the item from us we had just made. We spoke the ritual line of Inanna's, *What is this?* and received the unvarying answer, *Quiet, Inanna. The ways of the Underworld are perfect and may not be questioned.* For six days in a row I heard this spoken twenty times, one time each day for each woman. Not only that – I heard the *voices* of Inanna; her voices of outrage, shock, pride, fear, despair, dread, arrogance, beauty, power, hope and desperation varying through the days, through the women. I heard them coming out of my own mouth. I heard them traveling into the Underworld from where I stood in meditation, eyes closed on one or other side of the gate, waiting for each one of us to travel through.

I was going to write 'to travel safely through' but it wasn't safe. As we made each item of Inanna's regalia we meditated on what it meant to us. Thus Inanna's crown, for one woman, might be her job; or her inspiration; the achievements of her life; or her children. The breastplate might represent her security in the world; her beauty; the love she felt for and received from others; her health. The beads might be her singing voice; the threads that tied her to friends, family and community; or her hopes for the future. Those voices I heard, voices cracking, shouting, whispering – disbelieving, shocked, appalled – were the voices of women losing those things suddenly, unexpectedly. Her children. Her future. Her choices; her direction in life. Her lover; her creativity; her health.

My crown, on the first day, represented knowledge and I felt untouchable when they removed it, that nothing could break me. The small strand of beads on the second day was my voice, but I never spoke much anyway and I remained proud when they removed it. The third day's double strand of beads was my compassion and I felt even further isolated, estranged when I lost it. My breast-plate of the fourth day represented my vulnerability; that which allowed me to take a lover, to show myself to another and I felt only coldness when they lifted it from me. The fifth day's arm-band I thought of as my sexuality and fertility, bound together in that twisting of a snake along my arm. I felt a long way down, by then and it was a quiet horror to have it removed – I cannot keep even that, my birthright as a woman? – but I did not protest other than in the ritual words.

I remember I carried my measuring rod and line with magnificent pride. It represented my pen, my words; the actual lived power of my writing. To me it was magical, the power of my magic and I gave it a name; *My words are fire are blood are earth are star.* When they slid it upwards, out of my hand – so simple, so fatal – I could hardly breathe, hardly speak. It had not occurred to me while I was making or carrying it that I would lose it, or what that would mean. I had not even tried to hold onto it, to clutch at it. It was already gone, by the time I thought of it. The words came from me distantly; *What is this?* And I heard, inevitably; *Quiet, Inanna. The ways of the Underworld are perfect. They may not be questioned.* Then I tore apart.

For all my arrogance – this. For all my confidence, my pride, my self-containment, my delicate seclusion from the world – this. Utter loss. All that I had lost before, all that I had given away crashed down on me. Not just Inanna's regalia but all of my losses. Relationships, the agony of ill-health which I had suffered first with arthritis and then with RSI and glandular fever; the loss of friendships; opportunities; choices I had turned away from – all crashing down on me. Everything turning on the loss of my words, my writing. Are they so precious then – these little interfaces of mine with the world – that without this I am nothing?

In every Descent there is this point – *without this, I am nothing.* And then there is a pause, and the process continues. So I am not nothing, after all. So even beyond this loss, that loss, all losses imaginable, still I am, still I keep going. Recognizing oneself in this stripped form is an essential part of descending. *Oh. So I am still here. I cannot have been that thing that was me, after all.*

The following day I made my robe in silence.

Then I sat up that night, writing and meditating in a little space that had been set aside for us. The twenty of us were descending, one by one, into the night. We began as soon as it was dark and my turn came at about one in the morning. I had stayed awake. Others slept, or wept, or gazed inwards. Someone had coiled a thick rope into a spiral, spaced widely enough to walk. I had clothes, blankets, a light; I was in a daze with knowing this was the last of something. Other women came and went, meditated for a while, or slept and every twenty minutes or so one of us would be called to do her Descent.

It had occurred to me, somewhat dimly through the fog that had descended that the person behind all this, so to speak, was Ereshkigal and I was going to meet her. I went back and checked the myth; certainly Inanna met with Ereshkigal. She would be there and I – in the guise of Inanna – would be there. I could ask her what all this meant. I could hold her accountable for these actions and losses, and I intended to. I would demand an answer. I went through the gates full of purpose.

The temple was darkened, lit by candles. There was the sense of vague shapes, of purpose moving about in the background. There were seven gates, shrouded in draperies, constructed in the hall and at each one I was stopped.

What is this? I asked at each Gate; disdainful, righteous, fearful and each time was answered with, *Quiet, Inanna. The ways of the Underworld are perfect. They may not be questioned.* On I swept, through gate after gate, knowing I was going somewhere, imagining the answers lay just ahead. I would ask Ereshkigal what it meant. Why she was doing this. When they removed my robe at the last gate I crawled through, naked and bowed low, as it says in the story. As I began to stand I caught sight of Ereshkigal, distant on her throne in the dim light and I opened my mouth.

DESCENTS IN OTHER MYTHS

Persephone

Of Persephone's story, nothing is told of her Descent. This is mysterious, since much is made of the method of descending in other Greek myths; that of Psyche and also those of the musician Orpheus, and the adventurer Odysseus. The Greek Underworld has some well-known territory; the river Styx, the ferryman and the three headed guard dog Cerebus. Looking at Persephone's story more closely a great deal of emphasis is put on what happens in the upper world (frolicking in meadows, etcetera); and when Persephone disappears the emphasis remains in the upper world, with Demeter mourning, trying to find out what's happened and causing the first winter. There are whole long side branches of this story also, and they all follow Demeter. The last part of the story is again slanted towards Demeter; the spring that arrives is her joy at her daughter's return, rather than created by Persephone.

What happens on Persephone's journey into the Underworld, or while she is actually down there is shadowy, to say the least. The lack of explanation means we can begin understanding it fresh, rather than be pulled this way and that by a version which insists on motivations and emotions that, as we go deeper, we often come to question. It also makes the point that we can't, really, know what happens for someone else in the Underworld. To onlookers it always remains mysterious and perhaps essentially inexplicable. But in most stories there's at least a few events or actions described, from which to begin exploring. Not here – zilch. She was picking a flower one minute, vanished the next. Vanished literally from her own story.

What happens when we vanish from the story of our own lives? Death is the most obvious and complete vanishing, but there are other vanishings as well. Those times we turn almost into an auto-woman, just carrying out the actions expected of us as we sink into deep depression, or conduct a secret life elsewhere (even inside our heads) or wait, patiently, for things to change (even if they've been this way for years and show no signs of changing, or only of getting worse). We might vanish from the sight of others – allowing no-one to see what is truly happening for us – but of course we have not vanished from ourselves. We know our own stories, however reluctant or unable to tell them we might be. And I'm sure the Dark Goddess, in her cavern below, has her eye on us.

As anyone will know, who has become suddenly and severely sick and thus removed from her everyday life – or who has traveled overseas extensively before returning; or who has submerged themselves in a life-consuming love affair – when you come back, things are much as usual. All those things you were doing in order to keep the world turning; someone else has done them, or they remain undone and either way the world didn't even hesitate in its turning. Disconcertingly, when we vanish from the story the story keeps going. This is what happens on the face of Persephone's story – she vanishes and the story settles back on Demeter; whose story perhaps it has really been all along. It is worth considering that Persephone was barely a person on her own prior to her Descent, and the story's neglect of her, supposedly the central character, reiterates this. Only when she comes back does she display a name, a role, an individual purpose. She acquired them in the hidden part of the story. So obviously what happened down there is crucial.

I have tried to follow Persephone down.

Imagining Persephone

I am Persephone. I am walking down, into the dark. I thought that I would be alone, but my fear is still with me. The further I go into the rock of the earth the more animal it becomes. I have tamed my fear enough so that it walks by my side; before I set forth it was leaping in front of me. The earth and her dark wet air seem to press against me. With every step I decide to go in.

When Persephone leaves the daylight and her mother to travel into her self she does not carry a light. She does not believe that she will emerge again. She is not resolved about what she leaves behind and it is a mystery that she walks towards. Her mother is mourning her and although they say that Hecate stood by and watched her descend, no-one forgives what she is doing. Persephone is enacting her own truth. She is going in.

Speak to me Persephone, of your journey down; of the long winding passages of rock and stream that you forced yourself though. Tell me of the conviction that you held, even through the fear, of what you must do. How did you find your paths? And your choice, to embody dark and night, the inner earth; how did you accept death beyond life? Do you forsake yourself to bring the balance or do you, as I suspect, embrace it wholly; celebrate the death-aspect though you were the daughter? No wonder your mother weeps, to survive you.

I am Persephone. I breathe fear. I was not ready to leave the forests, the fields and yet I left them. I am lonely without my friends, my mother and yet I seek out other company, the dark spirits. I have forsaken the sun and the stars, yet they will find me again in the earth's jewels and her fires. I will meet the underground river. I am going in to the inwardness. I have left everything behind to find out who I am.

This journey of Persephone's is not over. It starts again with every woman who, looking over her shoulder at what she leaves still leaves on the journey that will take her into the unknown. Each woman that begins it for herself begins it again. It is always beginning. It begins as each woman learns that Persephone did not wait to descend without fear and that she, also, must descend with fear by her side. In the Underworld of our selves we can discover what we need to return. (Extract from 'Dancing the Red'; Jane Meredith.)

Psyche

Psyche's journey into the Underworld, unlike Persephone's, is well-documented. She had already been softened up for this journey by her previous three tasks for Aphrodite. But the fourth and final task assigned to her is the most impossible of the lot. She is told to go into the Underworld and ask the Queen of the Underworld, Persephone herself, for a box of her beauty ointment.

At each point in her journey so far – as each task was assigned to her – Psyche's impulse was to kill herself, rather than attempt it. Robert Johnson in *She: Understanding the Psychology of the Feminine* reminds us that this can be a metaphor for being willing to step away from our known life, up until now, and that each stage of our development in fact requires that we do this. It is also a precursor to Psyche's entry into the Underworld, the realm of death; all along, she has been willing to go there. Nonetheless it's hard not to get irritated at her apparently defeatist attitude. But then we should ask; how do I respond when I am handed the next (impossible) task by the Goddess? Perhaps we could learn something here.

Psyche receives advice and instruction from both the tower she has climbed and the reeds growing at the bottom of it. Perhaps Psyche has opened her awareness to the gateway to the Underworld by the nearness of her own death, in her readiness to throw herself from the tower. This is echoed in Philip Pullman's modern myth *His Dark Materials*, where Lyra has to discover a way to the Underworld. She does this by luring and then 'catching' her own death, using the simple technique of placing herself in mortal peril. She then forces her captured death to take her to the land of the dead.

Psyche is told she must carry two pieces of barley cake (or bread), and two coins and that she must help no-one along the way. The barley cake is to distract the three headed guard dog both on the way in and the way out of the Underworld. The two coins are to pay the ferryman, one for each direction. The warning about not helping anyone on the way reminds us that in some tasks we must remain very focused and may even appear to be selfish, or we will never complete what we have begun.

Psyche must pass beggars, whose hunger she could relieve by sacrificing one of her cakes or one of her coins; people who ask her to stop and help them and finally even a drowning soul in the river that she cannot assist.

In Psyche's journey into the Underworld, unlike both Inanna's and Persephone's; focused, continual choices are called for. I think the differences in these journeys of Descent are telling. Sometimes one disappears suddenly and dramatically from ordinary life – as Persephone did. Sometimes one arrays oneself in all one's powers for the journey, only to be progressively stripped of them as one descends – like Inanna. And sometimes – like Psyche – one has to keep focusing, sacrificing and staying on task.

RITUAL: SURRENDERING TO YOUR LIFE
The intention of this ritual is to accept all that has happened to you so far, and to begin to see your life as a whole.

Time: 1 - 2 hours; this can be split into two sections
You will need:
- Journal, or paper and pen
- A large piece of paper (or art paper or cardboard) for the mandala
- Objects for a mandala – appropriate art materials if you are going to draw; personal and/or found objects if you are creating a three dimensional mandala (further instructions below)

Part 1: Saying Yes
Good or bad, excruciating or ecstatic, the experiences you've had so far in your life are what have formed you. By accepting them, acknowledging them and then studying them you can be released to continue your journey.

It's often said that the only thing you can change is your own mind; or that the one choice you always have is how you interpret what happens to you. This ritual is designed to give you some freedom from, and acceptance of your past. Journeying to the Dark Goddess we cannot take anything with us and anything we try to take will only slow us down. And – perversely – we seem much more willing to leave behind – or let go of – happy experiences than unhappy ones. Seeing all of your past as meaningful, and having shaped who you are will assist your path into the Underworld and towards meeting the Dark Goddess.

- On two pages of your journal – or two loose sheets of paper – divide each page into two columns. Label the columns on the first page *Positive Events* and *Acceptance of Positive*. Label the columns on the second page *Difficult Events* and *Acceptance of Difficult*.
- In the column *Positive Events* write down all the wonderful things that have happened to you in your life (or as many as you can fit in!) These don't have to be in chronological order – just however they come to you. They might include the circumstances of your birth; your childhood and education; your gifts and talents; characteristics or values you embody; significant relationships; experiences and understandings. You don't need to describe them, just list them.

Sometimes people have difficulty recognizing what is good in their lives; particularly when they are in a very bleak place. If this is happening to you, imagine you are someone else, looking at your life. What would this other person say were some of the wonderful things in your life? Maybe it's the culture and time you were born into; maybe it's your intellect, sense of humor or deep understanding; maybe it's that wonderful connection you had with your teachers at school; your joy in dancing; the children you've loved.

Do not progress with this exercise until you have managed to fill up this column with wonderful experiences and events in your life, even if you have to put this exercise down and continue another day, or ask someone else for help. Only when you have completed this first column should you continue.

- In the column *Negative Events* write down all the difficult, painful and awful things that have happened to you in your life (at least the most significant ones). These could include illnesses; periods of depression; times of unemployment or uncertainty; relationship break ups; losses and deaths; addictions; accidents; personality traits you're not proud of; or things you were born with, or born into. Once again, they don't have to be in chronological order, or order of importance and you don't need to describe them in any way. Just list them. If you are having difficulty finding things to write in this column, you might imagine what someone else would say about your life.

- The column *Acceptance of Positive* is for you to record your acceptance of each of the wonderful things in your life on your list; regardless of whether they are due to luck, merit, hard work or someone else's love for you. Read the first item on your list and spend a moment really taking it in and feeling what it means to have, or to have had, that in your life. Reach out to it with a deep acceptance and when you feel that acceptance, write YES in the *Acceptance of Positive* column, next to that item.

- Move onto the second item and deal with it in the same way. Follow through with all the items on this list.

- Now look at the column called *Acceptance of Difficult*. It is for you to record your acceptance of the difficult and painful things in your life you have listed; regardless of whether they are due to bad luck, circumstance, your lack of effort or ability or someone else's actions. Read the first item on your list and spend a moment really taking it in, feeling what it means to have, or to have had, that in your life. Reach out to it with a deep acceptance – you do not have to accept that it was good to have this in your life, but just acknowledge that you DID or DO have it in your life. When you feel acceptance, that this is or has been part of your life, write YES in the *Acceptance of Difficult* column, next to that item.

Move onto the second item and deal with it in the same way. Follow through with all the items on this list.

There may be some items on this list you have a hard time writing YES next to. Remember you are not being asked to accept the value or merit of these things – simply that they are (or were) a part of your life. Writing YES next to them does not signal your approval, simply your acknowledgement that these things are included in the total of your life, with all their pain, difficulty, grief and disruption.

When we accept what is real and what has happened, we are able to integrate it. While we still seek to deny or hide from it, it's as if we are stuck there, staring at that very thing we most hate. Try it. If need be, you can refer back to your first list. Seeing the fullness and beauty listed there, you may be able to better acknowledge that hard things come into all our lives, but they do not negate the power or truth of the wonderful things.

Part 2: Seeing the Whole: Making a Mandala

A mandala is a design, usually circular and often geometrical or repetitive (but not always). It symbolizes the universe, or the whole. Mandalas visually represent your interpretation of a topic. They can be entirely free-form but they often begin with a structure, (such as dividing the circle into a certain numbe segments), which is then filled in.

Making mandalas, and later contemplating them, can be method of meditation, enquiry and reaching towards the divine. Mandalas are a way of both distilling and encrypting information (which can be feelings or thoughts) so that you can see more deeply into yourself. It is amazing how something you yourself created can teach you so much about how you think and your own experience. Creating mandalas you concentrate mainly on the details; in looking at them afterwards, you see the whole and that whole can be quite startling.

Anyone can create a mandala. The simplest way is to draw a circle – at least on an A4 piece of paper, but larger if you have one – and divide it into sections. The number and placement of sections will be relevant to the topic of your mandala. If you wanted to create a mandala representing light and dark it might simply have a line drawn through the middle, horizontally. If you wished to create one representing the seasons you would divide it into four quarters. A more mutable design might be the phases of the moon and you might choose to make the lines out from the centre curved, rather than straight, to represent the curving edge of the moon. The number of segments would depend on whether you chose to depict the moon's cycle as four phases, nine phases or twenty-eight.

There's another way to create a mandala and that is a 3D mandala. I've often done this outside; on the beach, in the garden or in a forest using found or brought objects. On the beach I draw out the circle and the dividing lines, and fill the sections with sand sculpture (usually abstract) and shells, seaweed, feathers – whatever I can find. In the forest I might use sticks as dividers for the circle (or you can use rocks or whatever you can find) and place a blanket of leaves over the whole, perhaps arranged by gradation of color or by type. I might add only a few objects – maybe seedpods or flowers. In the garden I've made mandalas with food – spaghetti is great for dividing the segments – and I use lentils, split peas, pasta, rice and other grains to fill in the mandala. You can place flowers, cut fruit and candles into the mandala. I then leave this – apart from the candles – for the birds and animals, as an offering.

You could also create a 3D mandala inside, on your altar for instance. Divide the altar into the appropriate number of segments – these could even be on different levels, depending on the structure of your altar – and then place meaningful objects into each section. If you do construct one of these 3D altars, consider taking a photo of it before you leave it or dismantle it. You can paste the photo into your journal and have it for further reflection.

Creating Your Ritual Mandala

- To begin with you may like to light a candle, or spend some time breathing quietly and centering yourself. Cast a circle or use some other method of preparation to enter a focused, sacred space. When you are ready, begin.
- On a page of your journal or a piece of paper list the sections of your life, chronologically. For example my sections might be: Childhood; adolescence; early-to-mid twenties; late twenties (which includes having a baby); thirties; forties up until now. (You don't have to do it in decades; for you, something else may be a significant divider, such as countries you've lived in or professions you've followed.)
- Count the sections of your life you have listed. This is how many segments your mandala will have (so my mandala would have six segments).
- It's also possible to create a mandala representing particular things – important moments in your life, the Descents you've made to the Underworld or anything else – but for this exercise, cover the entirety of your life so far.
- Now begin creating your mandala. Draw or mark in the

outer boundary and divide the mandala into the number of segments you require, of roughly equal size using lines radiating out from the centre.

- Start with the first period of your life you have listed. Choose which segment to place it in and – allowing yourself a light mind, so you can select colors, shapes or objects by intuition, without a whole lot of critical thinking or trying to 'get it right' – begin filling the segment in.
- You may choose to fill the entire segment, or to place a few items, drawings or shapes into it, leaving the rest empty. Do whatever seems best to you.
- When it feels complete for the moment, move onto the next segment and the next part of your life on your list.
- Continue, until you have completed the whole mandala.
- Glance over the mandala – there may be a segment that looks unfinished to you, in which case you can add something more. Sometimes people write words around the edges of the mandala or create a boarder around it.

When you've finished you might want a break for a few minutes, to stretch, drink some water or close your eyes. Then come back to your completed mandala.

- Study the mandala as if you were seeing it for the first time. Notice the colors of it. Notice how the segments relate to each other – whether they flow together, reflect or mirror each other or are completely different. Notice themes that reoccur, or segments that really stand out from the rest.
- In your journal or on some paper record your observations and what you think they might mean, as a reflection of the life you have lived until now.
- Come back to this mandala in a week or a month, and see what other understandings you receive from it. An interesting thing to do is to ask someone else; perhaps someone

who knows you quite well; to 'read' the mandala. Just ask them to comment on what they see, without knowing anything more than it represents the life you have lived. You will probably find at least some of their comments startling, insightful and supportive.

THE WAYS OF THE UNDERWORLD

As Inanna descends through her seven gates she constantly asks one question; *What is this?* It does not seem to matter that the reply does not answer her question, or that it is the same each time. Still, she has a need to question. The one piece of information she does receive is, *The ways of the Underworld are perfect.* We might ask ourselves what this means, as we struggle with various aspects of our own Descents. Perfect? All this loss and pain, difficulty and confrontation? Perfect?

It is only afterwards, looking back, that we usually have any hope of appreciating this type of *perfection*. When we perform a ritual Descent, we create this *perfection* for ourselves; perfectly matching each sacrifice with our ability to continue descending. When it happens in real life, and our losses are not controlled by us, it can be very, very hard to admit their perfection. In some cases, we simply may not be able to do so.

A woman I knew witnessed the sudden death, in a car accident, of her young daughter. I don't think words can convey the depths of her grief and pain. To me she seemed incredibly brave, confronting what this loss meant to her again and again; continually revisiting the internal places of her suffering. Several years after the event she was able to be deeply and genuinely grateful for the life of her daughter, regardless of its ending. Seven or eight years after that I heard her speaking again, and this time she spoke of a frame of mind I can barely imagine and I think most people would never reach. She spoke of the perfection of her daughter's death. It was particular to her, how she had understood it; and very personal. It didn't lessen her anguish or loss or missing of her daughter. But she had found a place where it made sense.

A tragically common experience many women have is to be adults still suffering the effects of childhood abuse and incest. Obviously this was never the choice of the child. Similarly, the adult woman would never have chosen to have such an experience, or to wish it on any child. But – if it has happened – she can come into a place where she accepts that it happened. Not a place where she accepts that it was good, or needful or even inevitable; but simply that it did happen, it is part of her history and part of who she is. Perhaps she has become a woman who is still battling with abuse, now in an adult relationship. Perhaps she has become an artist, or a dancer. Perhaps she has become a mother; a lesbian; a world traveler or a political activist. Within these contexts of her current life she may be able to see how the events that happened in her childhood have been part of shaping her; her strengths and understandings, as well as her weaknesses and pain.

Even beyond this acceptance some of these women have reached a place of understanding about the origins of abuse; whether that stemmed partly from alcoholism, a generational cycle of abuse, poverty, despair or a love expressed entirely inappropriately. This is not in any way to forgive or condone incest or child abuse or its perpetrators. It is a way of reclaiming some power and integration for the adult, who is no longer as helpless as they once were. Not every woman who experienced these things as a child will even want to confront them, or resolve them within herself to any degree. But I suspect anyone doing a Descent will have to look at them again, at least to the extent that they have come to partly define who she is.

Inanna is showing you can question all you want. But the questioning does not change the reality. In Inanna's story, questioning the Underworld is fairly pointless. The correspon-dence of that is to realize that arguing; prevaricating; refusing to

take responsibility; playing victim or 'poor me
blind; projecting or blaming and denying do n
on what is going on.

The ways of the Underworld are simple (as we
you will lose, give up or leave behind something of \   , ou
at each juncture. This will allow you to move forward. ...1e things
you lose will be the props; the supports; status; images; self-
beliefs; patterns of behavior and defenses you hold most
precious. Let's examine that. *The ways of the Underworld are
perfect*. That is, each thing that is removed from you is the exact
thing preventing you from descending. Perfectly. These things
are perfectly balanced, perfectly executed.

If, for example, I am operating under a belief that I am an
innocent victim, I cannot get any further into the Underworld
until I relinquish that. Event after event will conspire to show me
this is not the truth, not the whole story, not the belief I need
right now. Only when I let go of that belief – and exactly in the
letting go of it – will I be able to move forward towards a deeper
understanding of myself. Further, it will be the letting go of that
belief that allows me to go a level deeper, further towards my
truth and the naked rawness of my soul.

To descend into the Underworld and to meet the Dark
Goddess you must be ready to want that beyond anything. You
must be so determined (Inanna) or so desperate (Psyche) or so
carried away (Persephone) that you will be prepared to make
yourself sacred, sacrificing all that *appears* essential to you, as
you discover your real essence. Each gate shows you clearly
what you have to let go of, in order to move through. Each loss
will grant you an ability to move forward. That is, an Inanna still
wearing her crown must stay forever in front of the First Gate.
Inanna on the other side of the First Gate is *whoever she is without
that crown*. The loss of her crown doesn't just enable her transit
through that gate, or pay for it; the loss of her crown literally *is*
the movement through the First Gate.

The ways of the Underworld are perfect.

A SAMPLE DESCENT: GOING DOWN

For weeks, even months I have been trying to talk to my partner about difficulties I am having in our relationship. He's not interested. He tells me it's my problem, that he doesn't want to talk about it. He says it has nothing to do with him. Sometimes he tells me what's wrong with me, and what he thinks I should do to fix it.

I've been in despair, feeling so damaged in it I hardly know where to turn or how to think about it. Before that I was patient, waiting for him to express interest or concern. Sometimes I've been desperate, sobbing again and again, as if I can't get to the end of it. In between all that I've been pragmatic, telling myself that no relationship is perfect and this lack of communication, this somehow mysteriously being *on my own* with my problems is the fault with this one.

One particular morning I think there is a glimmer of hope, as he describes a dream of seeing a flower on a bush that he knew would fix things. I am excited by the dream and it seems to me a concrete suggestion. I ask if he will choose a flower essence for us both to take. *Fix yourself,* he says brusquely, perhaps interpreting my request as some sort of accusation or demand, and he leaves out the door on his way to work.

Fix myself. Well, that's something I know how to do. Hearing those words I feel as if I have been holding back for ages, waiting for him to want to come on the journey with me but he doesn't and I can't wait any longer. I don't have to wait, he's given me permission to get on with it, by myself. It is almost a relief, through my tears, to think I can finally deal properly with this rising alarm, this fear and hurt and stifled expression of mine, which I have tried to keep down as a way of avoiding upsetting him too much; confronting him; being difficult; awkward; demanding; emotional.

Now I will be all those things, but only with myself. I will unleash the Dark Goddess. There's only one way for me and it's shining ahead; the gates of the Underworld themselves. Descent. The path I know, that I've hesitated to take. This is my *marriage* after all, why would I put it on the line? I have resisted. But now it seems the only direction that holds out any promise, though of course I have no idea what that promise is. But I know it will shift me from this state and bring me through to somewhere new.

Leave a piece of myself behind, at the First Gate; I remember to do that. Ninshubur, my loyal retainer. It's myself, my calm and rational self; at forty-four surely I have won that. I pass her by in a blur, so urgent seems the need to get on with it.

The First Gate – my most precious belonging. There's no question in my mind about what that is. I take off my wedding ring and drop it into the chalice on the altar. Tears are pouring down my face. But the Dark Goddess has lent me ruthlessness and precision and I do not hesitate even for an instant. The ring has a gold snake twisting like a river through the roughened silver terrain. Alchemical; the male and female, the joining. If you put it on a table or a piece of paper the bottom sits flat to the surface, while the top is like a mountain range. It looks like a crown. I've always thought that, from the first moment I saw it.

I relinquish my marriage. My crown ring, my crowning glory. Inanna's crown. Oh, I found my beloved and – even – we married. A union of souls, of bodies, of love. A great hope. But I cannot carry it any further in this form. I lay it down.

To imagine my life without the relationship – I am doubled over, sobbing with intensity and grief. Oh, to have failed again. To give up, now. To discover the cup is empty, after all; the ring a meaningless symbol. Pulling it off my finger I was stabbed with the thought that I may never put it on again. And it was so beautiful. The sum of my achievements, of my quest for love. I am without it. It's like tearing myself apart, to relinquish it. I am leaving behind my dreams. And leaving you behind, who I committed to journey with. There is no other way forward.

It takes me about twenty minutes to recover enough to keep going. The ritual of this thing, of taking off the wedding ring, of beginning a Descent is so strong it has consumed me already. I am crying as violently as if I had literally torn him out of my life and would never see him again. This is only the First Gate and already I feel I am plummeting downwards, already I am partly unrecognizable to myself and the process is so ferocious I cannot imagine ever emerging. I do not look at the chalice on the altar. I do not really think of the ring as mine, anymore. I have lost it.

I have to keep going, I know I have only just begun. I have to go through the Second Gate, where Inanna gives up her jewels. My second most precious thing is another relationship. My son, nearly grown, who has been the star in my universe. Amazing, all I could ask for. Charming and intelligent and loyal, the person who knows me almost as well as I know myself. My traveling companion through years, the one I taught how to think and be in the world and then released gradually, step by step to find his own way. So many beautiful attributes he is carrying, a sense of determined happiness and equilibrium I have never had; a reflective sensitivity and honesty I've encouraged; a creative and critical engagement with the world I've nurtured. His life is the string of jewels about my neck, sparkling and precious.

If I died now, he is seventeen and would be all right. Not perfect, but strong and true. He is growing up anyway, it's nearly his time to leave so even though I love him endlessly, I can let him go. May life deal with you gently. And if he died now – if this is his death I am marking as I pass through this gate – well I have done it. Had the perfect child and given him over, to himself and the world. I lay it down. The crying still pours out of me, tearingly and probably endlessly; I will never get over this double loss.

Without either of them I am bereft but lighter. I feel simpler, rendered numb by emotion. Only about ten minutes pass in this second grief before I can keep going. I've lost all memory of what things were like before I began this process but that doesn't seem to matter. I'm alone in the house and no-one else will be here for hours. I could be anywhere by then. The phone rings and I ignore it. I feel nothing – distant, chilled, impossibly far away. I've left. I'm on the way down. I've left behind my two great loves and Ereshkigal is the only one who can reach me now.

At the Third Gate Inanna loses the double strand of beads that hang about her neck. For this I will sacrifice my order. The neatness of my life, knowing what comes next, how to deal with things. My daily lists; my patterning of the world; my under-standings of how things work; my way of fighting off chaos. The look of things – how good it looks; my partner, son, my work and house; the happy family. Inevitable after the first two gates, I could not hold onto it if I wished.

I lay it down, almost with relief. I do not have to understand things, to order them; I cannot manage anymore. I am past it, beyond it somehow and it is no longer my responsibility. I've failed and moved on. All that stuff I've been keeping under control – the house, garden, these relationships and our little order of life – I let it go. I breathe quickly, deeply. I'm hardly crying any more. Keep going.

The Fourth Gate and I am in a rhythm now. The breastplate. What is it that keeps me safe? Oh, this must be my defenses. That I can keep going, even under attack. That I can with-stand and with-hold and keep my centre and be okay, after all and after everything. That I have such a strong internal core it doesn't matter how I'm treated, what other people say or do. That I am defended in the world. Sane.

I lay it down. I will be the mad woman; the broken, crazy one. I will scream and screech and rend my face and tear my hair. I will be vulnerable, feel everything, every arrow aimed at me, all the suffering that comes my way I will not seek to hold it back it will sweep over, through me and I will be flecks on the surface of it, broken apart. I have no defenses, everything comes in at me all at once and I cannot hold together, any longer.

I have to rest after this. I have to fall apart. Not elegantly, but like atoms exploding. Violently. I feel depleted, desperate. The madness is already clawing its way in. I go to the kitchen for a drink of water and I choke on it. My left hand feels strange, the fingers touch together. No ring. Nothing there. I am heading into nothingness. I feel desperate, fast, free, wild, uncontained. I better get it over. I have not stopped crying but I scarcely notice it any longer.

At the Fifth Gate Inanna gives up her armband. I think of that armband as a sign of status. I know I am looked upon with envy sometimes. People consider I have achieved something in the world: success, happiness. I have the perfect child, perfect relationship, perfect life. I travel, I have a beautiful house. I can work at jobs I love passionately. I have stature, and status. When I arrange something – a ritual, a study group, a class or workshop – people come to it, with respect. I represent something for them. I've always thought it's because I carry an awareness that I am an aspect of the Goddess, and that's what they see, what they sense. It's what gives me my authority, my conviction, my strength. But now I lay it down.

I know the truth and I am not glamorous. I am not happy. I have not achieved the success I dream of. Here I am, a hollow woman on my knees, choking and sobbing not for losing this respect so much as what it represented to me; that I am on my own path, that I have stayed true to myself and the Goddess. Well, this is what's true down at the bottom of the Fifth Gate; I'm on the floor by my altar, with only two gates to go before the Dark Goddess. There's only me left, no others to win status or respect from, to join me in my ventures or approve of me or support me. I have stayed true to myself, but the rest I have thrown away; discarded; left behind. I'm on my way down and I can't carry anything with me.

At the Sixth Gate Inanna's lapis measuring rod and line is taken from her. It was used for measuring out the fields, for settling disputes. It was her authority. I've always had authority, the conviction of my beliefs. People think I know what I'm talking about. I think I know what I'm talking about, even when I'm making it up. I have a quick mind, I'm certain on my judgments. I have some base of certainty inside myself. From that comes forth ideas, strategies, opinions, actions. I can work, measure, count. I'm good at getting things done.

Now the idea that I could know what is happening, in any larger sense than this exact moment in the teeth of the Sixth Gate; the laughable idea that the future is mine to choose or that I have any power at all to effect the sequence of events in the world or even in my own life, I give up. My trust that I can read the signs, follow the way marked out for me, that I have any sort of a map or ability to make one – I lay it down. I am adrift on the dark breeze, a speck of dust blown towards the Seventh Gate. I stare at the floor. The draft of Underworld tunnels wafts me on, otherwise I might have stayed put for centuries; til I turned into dust myself.

But there's one thing left. It's the last, the Seventh Gate. Inanna had her robe taken from her here, or some would say, her life. I take off my clothes, slowly. It's hard to summon much focus. I'm reluctant to be cold, to be naked. Oh – this life. I remember it – that recognizable sense of it. My writing – relationship – place where I live – my cats – I have a picture of it, more or less. Being well, being alive – I remember it. Everything I wore in that life – this personality, this body – I lay it down.

I lie on the floor, on the carpet in front of the altar. It's rough. I'm cold. I've been crying so long it hardly counts, just tears leaking out of me by now, I can't summon any energy for it. It's taken two hours, this Descent and I don't recognize myself anymore. I am free of everything, past everything.

Ereshkigal; naked, weeping and bowed low I lay myself

before you.

Rip out my heart.

Claw my skin.

Hang me on the hook.

I have nothing, am nothing – just a body, greeting death. I give it all to you. My life, death.

I am yours.

Dream

I dreamed this fifteen years ago, or more. I was a priestess in a temple, perhaps I was even the High Priestess. Perhaps I was the Goddess herself. They came to me and they said, *Will you give everything?* And I said, *Oh yes, everything*.

Will you give up your studies, they asked; *Your learning?* And I said *Yes*.

Will you give up your friendships, your activities, your interests? Yes, I said; *Yes*.

Will you give up relationships, they asked; *Sex and comfort and sensuality? Yes*, I said.

Your lover, the father of your child? Yes, I answered, grandly.

And your son, will you give him up? That cut in hard, I had somehow not expected that. But I saw it was inevitable, it was what must be done. There was no other answer. Who was I, mortal, to think I could hold another life to mine? *Yes*, I said, though for the first time I wavered. I wondered what it would be like without him; if I would ever get him back.

And the lower levels of the Priestesses, they said; *Will you give them up?*

Yes, I said and watched them vanish from my knowledge, from my realm and my influence.

And the second ranks of Priestesses, will you give them up also? Yes, I said, measured; as if it mattered. *Yes I will.*

And the upper ranks, they asked, will you give them up also? And that hurt, surprisingly. That was like going into darkness; they were the shining lights. But there was no way to go but through and so I said *yes*, though my heart was not in it; I did not want to give them up.

And the highest of the High Priestesses, and the temple itself, they said; *Will you give all that up?*

And I said *yes* and was drowned on the instant into a swirling vacuum of blackness. Nothing was left but the tiniest speck of my consciousness, which meant almost less than nothing; I could hardly regard it.

That is well, they seemed to say, or I thought they might have said, in a distant universe. *That was well done.* But I had lost everything and no longer knew enough to even feel it.

RITUAL: A SEVEN-FOLD DESCENT

The intention of this ritual is to journey into the Underworld.

Please note: *If you take mood-altering drugs (prescription or otherwise), are receiving psychiatric treatment or have been diagnosed with a psychiatric illness, it is not advised that you undertake this ritual.*

Time: 2 – 3 hours, plus recovery time
You will need:
- Journal or a pen and paper
- Drawing things (optional)
- A place that feels safe to you– whether it's by the altar in your living room, at a friend's house, in a counselor's office or outside in a place special and sacred to you
- Someone to check in with (as you begin the ritual) and check out with (as you end it)
- Tissues can be useful
- A blanket or other covering
- Your altar and/or your offering/s to the Dark Goddess; at the very least a candle
- If you like, you can work with seven objects that have

power and meaning to you (further details below)

- Read through all of the Preparation for this ritual (below) well before you begin the ritual, even several days beforehand

Preparation

In this ritual you will discard all you have previously known, understood and been attached to. You may have a particular motivation for making this Descent, or you may be doing it as an exercise for learning, or as an offering to the Dark Goddess. Another purpose may be to resolve a difficult, painful or debilitating situation. It is of great assistance to be clear on your purpose for undertaking it (your intention) and to record this; in your journal, for instance.

Read through and complete the preparations prior to commencing the ritual, preferably a day or two before. Decide before you begin how long you will spend in the Underworld. You can spend three days, or three nights there as Inanna does; you can spend a week there if you feel you want more time or even a whole moon's cycle. There is a matching ritual on page 205 that will bring you up, out of the Underworld. It is not designed to be done immediately after this ritual, but after the length of time you have decided to spend in the Underworld elapses.

Perhaps you feel you've been caught in the Underworld for a long time and you want to do a ritualized Descent to acknowledge it, and hopefully find some way of moving on. Perhaps you've done Descents in the past – consciously or unconsciously – and are intrigued by the idea of making a map of your experience, or of exploring the terrain in a different way. Perhaps you just have a pull towards it, a yearning; to begin to make sacred, or make sense of this idea of descending, of meeting the Dark Goddess. You might be one of those women who has always been drawn towards the myths and Goddesses of Descent. Perhaps you think it is important work that should be regularly done, until we lose our fear of it and it becomes no more remarkable to us than any other spiritual work.

However you've arrived here, there are some things to do before you undertake a ritualized Descent; even – or especially – if you feel you are trapped somewhere in the Underworld. Putting into effect the proper procedures of a Descent can greatly aid you in orienting yourself, in making sense of the process and in understanding how to move forward.

I believe fundamentally and absolutely that Descents are meant to be undertaken, that we are made to journey these paths. But I cannot say it is entirely without risk; to your emotional stability, for example; or your current way of life. Part of the sense of danger we experience descending to the Underworld is because of the neglect, ignorance and fear we have around the process. Our lack of practice makes us clumsy in it. Also, because we do not undertake regular Descents there is a resultant backlog effect, with all the pressure coming though at once instead of being released incrementally, or addressed on a regular basis. All these things add together to make Descents appear more dramatic, possibly more dangerous and even more intense than they might be, were we to live in a different world where this was just part of what everyone did and you had been taught since adolescence exactly how to do it.

The Check-In Person

Choose a check-in person. This is someone you check in with, before you begin this process, and then check out with when you finish it, even if it is not immediately (later that day would be fine, the following week would not be).

The check-in person should be someone you trust and who understands what you are doing. This person will be standing in for Ninshubur, though you should also put an internal Ninshubur on alert. Before you begin the ritual, talk to your check-in person. This doesn't have to be the minute before you begin, it might be the day before. Make sure you tell them what the process is, why you are doing it and also some practical details about how to bring you back to ordinary reality (rescue you) should you need it after the ritual.

If it were me I would tell my check-in person that eating, sleeping and exercise all help me to return to my body and the present time, so if I appeared vague, distraught or disoriented, they would check I had eaten, and suggest I could have a rest or take a walk. Another thing that helps me is writing things down, so they might suggest that I make notes of my experience and particularly any new understandings or insights. I find baths wonderfully soothing, and listening to certain music. If need be, there are several people (some professional counselors and wise women) I would trust to do a full debriefing of a ritual for me, and to literally pull me out of whatever stuck space I had got into. My check-in person should know who these people are.

Your check-in person could be your counselor, your friend, your priestess or anyone you trust to be reliable and stay grounded and practical. It may be someone who knows exactly what a Descent is, or just someone who respects your processes. It might be your sister or flat mate, but it cannot be your cat or your spirit guide. They may be very helpful at some stages of the journey but for this role you need a live human being, easy to contact and with enough attention to spare to hold this role for you. I have not listed a partner as a possible check-in person, though you should use your own judgment on this. It can be better to have someone with a greater degree of detachment to the outcome of your Descent than you would expect a partner to have.

The check-in person should know the times you are planning to start and finish your ritual and you should arrange, during the check in, a time that the two of you will check out. It is not enough for the check out to consist of, *Are you all right?* Schedule at least a fifteen minute check out and maybe longer. During this time you should force yourself to talk, to describe how at least some of the ritual was for you; some understandings or changes you reached; and how you will now proceed with the rest of the process.

If you find yourself reluctant – or unable – to speak of these things, you will know something is wrong. Hopefully your check-in person will also realize this, though most of us are very good at hiding such truths from others, and it can be particularly easy to do so on the phone. However, even though you have assigned this other person the role, it is really *you* who are your own Ninshubur, so even if they don't pick up on the fact that you're not all right, you still need to take responsibility for it. You may have thought you provided them that list of what they should suggest to you in such circumstances for their use; but no, you provided it to them so you would have to think it through and would have access to it when you needed it. Like now. You could even signal to them something is going on for you by saying something like *I think I'll take a bath,* so they will realize you are in need of grounding and comfort.

The Safe Place

Do this ritual somewhere you will not be interrupted and you feel sheltered and free to feel and express emotion. Descending to the Underworld is already an edgy business, don't exacerbate it by carelessness or bravado. *Oh yes, I'm used to coping; I'll fit my Descent into a half-hour before picking the kids up from tennis and making dinner.*

You may choose to do your Descent in your counselor's office, with the counselor as your check-in person; that's fine. You may choose to do it in a magical or ritual circle; either with other women who are also doing a Descent or by yourself. You may choose to do it in a place where you regularly hold ritual, or practice devotion, or meditation. You may choose your living room, a grotto, garden or orchard. I don't recommend bedrooms for Descents; or at least not the bed. Beds are best left for restful and loving experiences. You may choose a beautiful place out in nature, such as a waterfall, forest, beach, cave or mountain top.

If you have chosen somewhere wild or remote, be sensible about safety issues. Let several people know where you are going and when you will be back. It's best if you know the area well. Remember you may be disoriented or distressed during or after the ritual, and take helpful remedies with you; food, water and a blanket at the very least. You might even ask someone else to come with you to act as a guardian; they could wait by the car while you do your ritual, or you might prefer that they sat nearby and kept you in their sight.

The Mechanics of the Ritual
How you do this ritual is really up to you.

I am going to suggest one way, but if something else feels better – for example, I have suggested you make a visual or written record of each of the gates after you've been through it, but if you sense them most strongly *before* you go through, and would rather draw or write then – change the form of the ritual. With the exception of the final, Seventh Gate, let the objects (if you are using objects) and gates take on their own meaning. It will be different every time you do this ritual, and different for every person. The exception to this is the Seventh Gate, which represents your body, or your life; passing through it is a symbolic death, beyond which you have nothing left.

Mostly, the experiences of passing through one or two of the gates are more powerful than the others, but there is no knowing which gates these will be, or how any particular experience at any gate will take you. Begin with knowing you have seven to get through and make a commitment to yourself that you will complete all seven in the time you have allowed. Often after a very difficult gate, the next several are easier.

The aftermath of this ritual will be that you will spend time in the Underworld, with the Dark Goddess. You can plan for this to be three days (a traditional time and you may even choose to run this ritual over a dark moon) or you may like to spend a week or a month down there. The corresponding ritual, for Ascending back up through the seven gates to the upper world is in the third part of this book.

The Altar

Carrying through from your earlier work of honoring the Dark Goddess, use an altar for this ritual. Construct a simple altar if you are outdoors – a rock, a layer of leaf litter or a piece of swept sand – and on it lay any offerings or gifts you have for the Dark Goddess, whether these are from your previous work or are made especially for this ritual. If they are natural or bio-degradable you might choose to leave them there when you are finished.

Indoors you can make a new altar – on a box, table, shelf or piece of floor – with a cloth and your offerings, or continue to use one you have already set up; depending on where you are and your preferences. I have listed a candle as the very minimum required for your altar, though in some circumstances it may not be appropriate and candles always carry a fire risk and must never be left burning unattended. If you are outside it may be safer and more practical to have a beautiful flower, an arrangement of colored leaves or a handful of seedpods. For the Dark Goddess people sometimes place dark colored feathers, or even bones they have found of a bird, snake or other animal on their altars.

Optional – Seven Objects

If you like you can have seven objects with you to use in this ritual Descent. You can match them to Inanna's objects – crown, necklet, double strand of beads, breastplate, armband, measuring rod and line, and robe – or just choose seven objects that are both precious and symbolic in some way to you. I have always found that until I am in the teeth of the ritual I cannot know what each gate will come to represent, so if you are not replicating Inanna's seven objects, I advise just trusting that they will sort themselves out as it happens, as to which object will come to represent each gate.

Recording Your Descent
I find it is very useful to record some of the thoughts and under-standings – or it could be visions, pictures, or phrases of song or poetry – that go through my head *while* I am doing the Descent. The map-making segment, later, is vital to fix the procedure, process and generalized understandings about the Underworld, but this recording of impressions during the Descent is also precious. This might take no more than a minute or two at each gate, or you could spend twenty minutes or so recording your impressions at the end of the whole ritual. If you feel uncertain of how to express yourself, or to find words for this process, use pastels, charcoal or watercolors to make quick patterns, sketches or impressions of color, shape and emotion. You may choose to use a visual form of recording anyway, in preference to words, or have a voice recording device, or you may find poetry the best way to express yourself. Have the tools for this nearby.

The Ritual
To Begin the Ritual
I recommend beginning this ritual formally, with creating sacred space by casting a circle or using some other method, and then spending a few moments in stillness before making a dedication to the Dark Goddess.

Some people like to cleanse the space energetically before they begin a ritual. To do this you can use a smudge stick, incense or chimes (or a clear tone using your voice). You can use water with a few drops of essential oil stirred into it and sprinkle it around and on yourself. Think of the sound, the water or the smoke as purifying the space around you, clearing out any unnecessary distractions or influences and marking this place and time as sacred.

The simplest way cast a circle is to mark out the four compass directions – North, East, South and West (or as near as you can work out) – and, leaving you enough space to do the ritual within, walk to each quarter in turn and acknowledge that direction. This walk is performed clockwise in the Northern Hemisphere; anti-clockwise in the Southern Hemisphere. The associations for the directions in the Northern Hemisphere (beginning in the North) are usually: North – earth, winter and dark moon; East – air and spring and the waxing moon; South – fire, summer and full moon, West – water, autumn and the waning moon. Complete your circle by turning back to the North again. In the Southern Hemisphere begin in the South, with these associations: South – earth, winter and dark moon; East – air and spring and the waxing moon; North - fire, summer and full moon; West – water, autumn and the waning moon. Complete your circle by turning back to the South again. In each direction you can use words connected with these attributes; your own words or method of casting a circle; or simply stand silently for a while, establishing a connection and acknowledging that you stand within a circle.

There are alternatives to casting circles in order to create sacred space, and you should feel free to use whichever you are comfortable with, familiar with or suits you. You may prefer to drum or dance or draw a circle in chalk. If you don't normally create sacred space, try the circle casting method briefly described above. There are many books and internet sites that give much more detail should you wish for it.

Once you have created sacred space, attend to your altar. This may mean constructing it, placing an offering upon it, lighting a candle or just sitting next to it for a few moments, allowing your mind to still. Following on from this take a few more minutes to deliberately calm your breathing, attune your focus to within and become aware of your emotional, energetic and physical states.

Finally, speak – or whisper, or sing – your dedication to the Dark Goddess. This is when you name, aloud, why you are undertaking this ritual. You can keep it very simple, acknowledging the Dark Goddess and speaking your intention to come towards her. For example, *I wish to meet with the Dark Goddess.* It may be more elaborate or more specific, such as, *I'm ready to step into the place where I don't know anything.* Or, *Dark Goddess take me down into your Underworld to find myself.* Or, *Persephone, let me come and find you and learn what you learnt.* Let the words come as they will, by now you are moving into ritual space and not everything can be planned beforehand or controlled precisely.

The First Gate

Ask yourself what is dearest to you. What do you value the most, what have you been clinging to, what is your stumbling block? The answer will usually be obvious. If you have half a dozen possibilities flood into your mind, now is the time to exercise your truth and honestly acknowledge which of those things seems most precious to you right now, even if it is not a conventional answer or one you would admit to anyone else. It might be your children; your lover; your house; career; spiritual practice; creativity or something more ephemeral such as your freedom or your potential.

If you are using objects, choose an object to represent what you are giving up at the First Gate. If you are working with Inanna's objects, at the First Gate you lose your crown.

Now lay this thing down. If you are using an object, lay it on the altar. This is where you need to enter deeply into the ritual and believe, if only for a moment, that this most precious thing is gone from your life forever.

Feel its loss. Mourn it. Feel into yourself and discover what it is like to be without that. You might feel shock; devastation; grief; freedom; wonder; power; hope; there is no prescription for what you might feel. But it is crucial that you feel it, whatever it is. You might also visualize yourself as passing through a gate, crossing over a threshold or literally stand up and take a pace forward.

Afterwards you might like to drink some water, do some breathing exercises or record the First Gate in your journal. When you are ready, continue on.

The Second Gate

Ask yourself, from what remains in your life after the First Gate, what is most precious to you, what you value the most, what you cling to and protect and defend. It may be a relationship, an attribute of your personality or a part of your life such as motherhood, career or music.

If you are using objects, choose an object to represent what you are giving up at the Second Gate. If you are using Inanna's objects, at the Second Gate you lose your necklet.

Now lay this attachment down. If you are using an object, lay it on the altar. Feel what it means to you to remove this thing from your life. Feel it as fully as you can, knowing in this moment it is lost to you forever; you will never have it again. Feel all of the feelings associated with that loss and express them however you need to; you might weep, scream, shout, bang your hands on the ground or hold your body close.

You might also visualize yourself as passing through a gate, crossing over a threshold or literally stand up and take a pace forward.

Then feel who you are, now, without that thing you laid down.

If you want you can take some time to recover, and make notes in your journal.

The Third Gate

By now you may be entering into the rhythm of the ritual and know already what it is you will give up at the Third Gate. If not, ask yourself the question again; what is most precious to me; what do I love; what am I proud of; what defines me; makes me feel secure and certain? It may be your job, your friendships or your art. When you have the answer, continue.

If you are using objects, choose an object to represent what you are giving up at the Third Gate. If you are using Inanna's objects, at the Third Gate you lose your double strand of beads.

Now lay this thing down. If you are using an object, lay it on the altar.

Once again, feel the loss of this, mourn it and then feel into who you are now, without it. You can also visualize yourself passing through a gate, crossing over a threshold or if you prefer, stand up and take a pace forward.

Take a few moments to recover, to drink some water and make notes or a sketch if you wish.

The Fourth Gate

What is left to you? Powerful aspects of your personality (strength, caring for others, ambition, creativity); achievements (whether personal, spiritual or work-related) and certainties (such as owning a house, good health and secure employment) are all contenders to be relinquished. Choose what seems to you the most powerful thing to surrender, something whose loss will devastate you.

If you are using objects, choose an object to represent what you are giving up at the Fourth Gate. If you are following Inanna's pattern, at the Fourth Gate your breastplate is taken from you.

Now lay this thing down. If you are using an object, lay it on the altar. Imagine yourself passing through a gate, crossing over a threshold or else stand up and take a symbolic pace forward.

Go into the feeling of the loss of this thing you have relinquished. Feel how your life will be, without it. Imagine the consequences of being without it and who you might be, now. You can grieve; rage; laugh; shout; dance.

Before you go onto the Fifth Gate do some deep, slow breathing and if you have lost touch with your body, try to come fully back into it.

The Fifth Gate

Perhaps it is your dreams you will lay down now; your ambitions; desires or longings. Perhaps it is some worthy quality you have always aspired to and measured yourself against, such as loyalty; unconditional love; selflessness or integrity. Make sure it is something you deeply value, that you almost cannot imagine yourself without.

If you are using objects, choose an object to represent what you are giving up at the Fifth Gate. If you are echoing Inanna's objects, at the Fifth Gate you lose your armband.

Now lay your chosen thing down. If you are using an object, lay it on the altar. Visualize yourself passing through the gate, crossing over the threshold or stand up and take a pace.

Register what you have lost. Feel whatever feelings arise to meet the loss. And then feel into yourself; who are you now, without this quality or this part of your life?

Take a moment to record any impressions or understandings you have in your journal. Check that you have a record of what you have let go of at each gate, so far.

The Sixth Gate

At the Sixth Gate you may feel to acknowledge a powerful quality that is generally perceived as negative, but that is still something that helps define you. Thus you might choose to relinquish your anger; your addictions; your pessimism or distrust. Or you might relinquish a heritage you have always held to –

cultural; familial; racial or religious. Only you can know what is powerful enough to hold you to the upper world, and therefore what must be let go of before you can descend fully. If you have kept a secret strength or hope alive until now, nursing it through the previous gates without giving it up, now is the time to be ruthless with yourself, and name it. It might be love, or hope, or faith.

If you are using objects, choose an object to represent what you are giving up at the Sixth Gate. If you are using Inanna's objects, at the Sixth Gate you lose your measuring rod and line.

Now lay this thing down. If you are using an object, lay it on the altar. Visualize yourself as passing through the Sixth Gate, or crossing a threshold. If you prefer, take a pace forward.

Acknowledge what you have let go of; all that it meant to you and perhaps even its limitations as well as its protections and value. Feel all of your feelings.

You may wish to take some time to recover or rebalance yourself before moving on. You can stand up and stretch or drink some water and close your eyes for a little, connecting with your breath and heartbeat. Write or draw in your journal if you wish.

The Seventh Gate

At the Seventh Gate you surrender your life, both this physical body that you have carried around the world and the life you have constructed for yourself with all its attributes. This is the place of utter surrender, for which all the other gates have been practice.

If you are using objects, your remaining object will represent your life. If you are working with Inanna's objects, at the Seventh Gate you lose your robe (your clothing).

Now lay this thing down. If you are using an object, lay it on the altar. Take all your clothes off, if that seems appropriate. Imagine yourself passing through this final gate, crossing the threshold. If you prefer, take a pace forward.

You might like to lie down, even on a blanket, or fold the blanket around yourself. Feel your death. One day it will come to you, and you can imagine that day now. What does it feel like to be leaving behind all you have known, all that you have constructed and all the people and things you have loved? To be leaving all suffering and pain and doubt? To be leaving this physical world; the beautiful earth with its sunrises and trees and birds and winds? To be leaving all physical experiences; eating and making love and growing and using your senses?

Allow yourself some time, past this Seventh Gate. You may pass into a very quiet, still place within yourself. You may need to process things, in which case you can make notes in your journal, and soon proceed to talking with your check-in person and taking any other actions you know will assist and support you.

You may spontaneously have a vision, or other experience of the Dark Goddess. In the next section of this book you will be led to meet with her, but it is possible she will come to you in the meantime. If this happens you can make the offerings you laid on the altar earlier, directly to her. You can thank her for being present, and tell her you've come to learn from her. Or you can just remain there, in your dead form, becoming the offering yourself.

Before you complete this ritual it is worth recording, at the very least, what each of the gates meant to you. If you experienced strong visions you might like to try drawing one or two of them, or if you heard voices or came to new understandings, you can write them down.

Completing the Ritual

This ritual leaves you in the Underworld. In the final section of this book, you will be guided on an Ascent ritual, to return to the upper world. Meanwhile, it is important to remember you will still be in the Underworld when you finish this ritual; for three days, a week or whatever length of time you have decided. You should still ground your circle and complete this ritual, although you can leave your altar as it is and come back to it for the next ritual, if that's practical.

To finish, or ground a ritual, you should do all of the things you did to begin it, in the reverse order. (Sometimes this is called 'opening' a circle – just to confuse things – which means you are opening it back to ordinary space. I prefer to use the terms 'casting' to begin and 'grounding' to finish, to avoid the confusion involved with the words 'opening' and 'closing'.)

Begin the grounding by acknowledging and thanking the Dark Goddess, even if you did not feel her presence very strongly. In a way, your experience with her is yet to come.

Then either dismantle or pack up your altar – or if you are leaving it there, blow out any candles and put out any incense that is burning.

Now ground (or complete) your circle or sacred space. If you cast a circle, ground it in the reverse order you cast it, that is North – West – South – East – (or in the Southern Hemisphere, South – West – North – East). You might like to say a few words in each direction, or simply stand in silence at each point, observing and acknowledging that direction.

Finally, do something to symbolize that the space you have used for your ritual is now ordinary space again – make a tone, or chime, or stamp your feet and wave your arms around.

After you've attended to your immediate physical needs, you should contact your check-in person at the time arranged, and do the check out. This is more fully detailed in the preparation notes, at the beginning of this ritual.

Over the following hours and days, remain aware of the depth and power of the ritual you have just completed and give yourself the support you need for whatever you are undergoing, whether that is mild curiosity, complete purging or deep understandings. If you need support beyond what your check-in person provides take responsibility for finding it, whether it comes in the form of sharing with friends; seeking out a counselor or appropriate self-help book or group; or taking time out for yourself. No-one else can decide what is right for you, and no-one else is responsible for finding or providing it. Think of taking these steps to support yourself, which may be very difficult or unaccustomed to you, as being the follow-through on your dedication to the Dark Goddess, at the beginning of this ritual.

MAKING A MAP OF THE JOURNEY

Before you move onto the next stage of this journey to meet the Dark Goddess, and the next part of this book, take some time to make a map of your Descent.

Often the Descent itself is the most emotionally charged of all the stages of a journey to the Underworld, so distilling what you have learnt into some form of map is invaluable. You might want to make this part of your map in seven distinct stages, mirroring the seven gates – seven verses of a song; or an actual map with seven gateways on it – or you might choose to emphasize other aspects of descending.

A map serves several purposes. One is the recording of what you have learnt; literally recording where you have been. Another purpose is as a guide, for yourself on any return trip or for anyone who comes after you. Because we have largely been in denial and avoidance about the Descents in our life; slow to acknowledge them, rarely finding appropriate resources or support and mainly wishing only to get out of them as soon as possible (though this very wish may end up prolonging the visit) we have rarely been conscious enough to make good maps. There is also huge stigma associated with depression, withdrawal and inner reflection beyond a certain point; enough to ensure that our experiences in descending and being in the

Underworld are not valued and our journeys rarely validated or examined in depth.

Even when we know ourselves to be descending we are rarely able to learn from our previous experiences, or from those of our mothers, sisters and best friends. Self-help books somewhat take the place of this in our world; they can be like a friend telling you of their experiences in the darkest places. Making our own maps we can better assist ourselves, those closest to us and – when we are bold enough to make them more widely available – we help make the whole concept more available and less shrouded in obscurity.

Writing

I love writing. For me, there's nothing as satisfying as a journal entry made at the time I was experiencing whatever-it-was. It's not just the words I've written; it's the style I've used – poetic and flowing, stark and abrupt or factual bullet points – that tells me so much about what it was like. My handwriting, also – sprawled across the page, tiny and clipped, neat and orderly or interrupted with diagrams and stray thoughts (sometimes blotted with tears) – adds to this picture.

If you want to experiment with writing, beyond straight journal-keeping, you could try creating a seven-versed ballad for your Descent. Or a series of haikus (a Japanese form of poetry kept strictly to seventeen syllables). You could try writing in flow-of-consciousness; or maybe a travelogue, with everything described in detail, for future travelers.

If you are using the journal form you may want to make a series of entries. There will be the notes you took while you were doing the Descent, in-between gates; then the notes you wrote at the end of the ritual. Come back to this in the next day or two and write in as much detail as you can about your experience. A week or so later, you can write an overview, as well as noting anything that has changed in your life, and decisions or actions you've taken as a result of your Descent. These snapshots of how you were feeling at different times and the progressive understandings you have reached help to make a more complete written map.

Dancing

You might choose – as well as, or instead of writing – to record your Descent some other way; in dance, for instance. The dance of the seven veils is believed to have originated with a telling of such a Descent.

You don't have to be a dancer to choose this option, just willing to move your body. You can find music that recreates the atmosphere of your Descent and the Underworld, make your own music or dance in silence. You might choreograph your dance; dance freely and spontaneously or evolve it over several sessions. You can have someone record your dance on video or with still photos; this will make more of a permanent map than a single dance performance. If you don't do this, make sure you find some other way to record it, whether with some words in your journal, or some sketches of the dance.

I am envisaging this as a solo dance, with no audience; but maybe you'll choose to make it a group piece, a performance piece or incorporate it into another ritual.

Instead of dance, you might write and perform a piece of music or a song as your map of the Descent you have undertaken.

Art work

You've already used art work in this book, to make your mandala. Even if you do not consider yourself any sort of an artist (and most of us don't), anyone can put color onto bits of paper. Crossing boundaries into mediums that are not your usual ones – getting out of your comfort zone – can increase your range of self-expression. Using color when you would usually use words can show you different things about the experiences you're recording.

For an art work depicting your Descent find a large piece of paper or card; the larger the better. Invest in some coloring materials (even if you have children, and therefore access to these, it's wonderful to have your own; unbroken, all colors present, kept in their own box...) Some people are happy with textas, others like crayons or oil pastels and personally I love the chalky type of pastels that blend so well. But maybe you will make a collage, or paint a wall, or use your computer to create an art piece.

Your art can be abstract; a cartoon; a literal cartographic-style map or representational. You may choose a different style of art altogether, such as sculpture, weaving or photography. Remember to capture some elements of mapping in your art, rather than purely a feeling or mood. Mapping assists you when you return, and it may even help someone else to find their way, on their own Underworld journey.

PART THREE:

IN THE UNDERWORLD

IN THE UNDERWORLD

Mysterious things happen in the Underworld. Death, obviously. Rebirth, eventually. Transformation, necessarily. Events and synchronicities occur in myths that are inexplicable according to upper world standards and procedures. We, the readers of the myth, can observe and wonder at them, but no rationale is provided. The Underworld, which we disappear into and emerge from, is a crucible for such happenings. Although these mysteries are pivotal to the development and conclusion of the myth, they do not have a simple or single explanation.

What happens down there is the business of life and death, of initiation and integration. But things in the Underworld do not stay neat or separate, you cannot have just one part of this. And – contrary to our beliefs – death can be gentle, while life is often abrupt, painful and conflictual. Birth and death are not separate from each other and this is obvious in Underworld mythology. They are points on a circular continuum, and much closer to each other than is comfortable for us to imagine. Not only must each thing that has been born come to death; life and death literally feed each other. From decaying compost new life sprouts. The rotting tree in the forest creates humus that will nurture the new, young trees. Our bodies, upon death, feed back into the earth, which recycles their components endlessly.

We all have direct, bodily experience of one part of this cycle already; being born. Many of us have given birth, in our turn. The one guaranteed event at birth is eventual death. Giving birth is therefore giving death, as well. Birth and death are part of the same cycle, brought about in the same moment. Inextricable, inseparable. How could we say that one is sacred and the other a depravity? How to say one is glorious and one inglorious? They are the same, as much as the in-breath is joined to the out-breath; they do not come separately and it is impossible to have one without the other.

Death and change are the business of the Underworld, and the non-debatable nature of this is in direct contrast to our cultural determination to stay always in the bright light of daylight; upwards and onwards. I believe that our experience of the severity of the Underworld is partly due to our current imbalance in our personal lives and in our culture regarding our inability, or unwillingness, to give the dark half of the cycle (winter; death; decay; initiation; transformation) its due. Its dangers, mysteries and gifts remain alien to us. Journeying to the Underworld – especially conscious journeying – provides us an opportunity to become more familiar with these dangers, mysteries and gifts.

Psyche is required to obtain a box of beauty ointment for Aphrodite from the Queen of the Underworld (actually Persephone). What kind of beauty does the Queen of the Underworld lay claim to that Aphrodite, whose beauty is legendary, does not already have? When Psyche opens the box of beauty ointment (against strict instructions) something rises up from it – a vapor, a mystery – and upon breathing it, Psyche drops dead. It is a danger, a mystery and a gift all in one, as we discover this beauty ointment is fatal to mortals. Perhaps Aphrodite bargained on that, when she assigned Psyche the task, or perhaps she was fulfilling her greater role – not as Psyche's tormentor but as her initiator – but either way, I think the box must have held something of value to Aphrodite. What was in that box? That's one of the Underworld's mysteries.

I have created day long rituals that follow Psyche's journey. In the mid-afternoon I've sat in the centre of an Underworld labyrinth as the Dark Goddess, a black silk veil draped over my body. I hand out tiny wooden boxes to all of the Psyches in the workshop, sometimes twenty or more. Religiously, each one asks me for a box of beauty ointment; some on their knees, some boldly and some with reverence. Carefully I give each one a box.

On receiving it they start their winding journey back to the upper world. At some point along the way they open the box, each one wanting – like Psyche, like me – to know what's in it. What did Persephone's box contain?

All I have put in it is a few drops of essential oil – something very earthy, smelling like compost – so basically it's an empty box. But they fall to the floor, echoing Psyche's death in the myth. When eventually I sound the chimes that signal Psyche's rescue, they rise and we form a circle.

I have asked them: *What was in the box? Did you discover what was in the box?* – and each woman has said yes, she knows now what was in the box. And then each woman has a different answer: *Love; my soul; death; completion; a sense of the Goddess; the unknown; peace...* So Persephone's beauty ointment remains a mystery, understandable by each woman in her unique circumstances but with no general rule that we can put on it. Perhaps it is just whatever you need to transform. And that precise thing, transformation, might be an attribute that Persephone holds and Aphrodite does not; a kind of regeneration particular to the Dark Goddess and associated with beauty, mortality and death.

Persephone herself, in her younger form, visits and also ingests something of the Underworld. She eats seven pomegranate seeds (or five, or some other number depending which version you're reading) and this action binds her forever to the Underworld. Perhaps you'll notice that, although she is allowed to return annually to visit her mother in the upper world, synchronistically she is granted this favor *after* she has eaten the pomegranate seeds. She entered the Underworld an innocent maiden and become the Queen there. She departed a very different Goddess than the one who entered the Underworld. What happened, exactly? What were those seeds? What transformation did they contain?

Again, I have done this as a ritual and watched one woman cramming the red seeds into her mouth, smearing the juice over

her face; while another woman carefully picks /
eats them delicately, naming each one; anothe
does it and another in a joyous ecstasy. So watcm...
I find that Persephone trembled; that she reveled; that si..
and laughed and cried. I find she was fascinated; compelled;
afraid; grieving; reluctant; ecstatic; eager and joyous. The
complexity of a myth is conveyed by the multiplicity of human
motivations and responses.

What does it mean, to eat the seeds of the pomegranate? What
does it mean to be bound to the Underworld? A simple interpretation is that the seeds are the seeds of life – literally – and eating
them symbolizes binding a woman into her reproductive and
mortal life. Persephone – synchronistically again, or it may be the
pomegranate was merely a euphemism – becomes pregnant to
her husband Hades, thus binding her doubly to her fate in the
Underworld. Ingesting the red seeds of the pomegranate and
receiving the generative seeds of her lover into her womb are
nicely parallel actions.

Inanna, in her story, hangs on a meat hook for three days and
nights while Ereshkigal is apparently in labor, moaning and
groaning alone, until Inanna's rescuers arrive. Interestingly, the
only way they can rescue Inanna is to firstly rescue Ereshkigal, at
least from her isolation. Does Ereshkigal actually give birth, and
if so, to what or whom? Maybe Ereshkigal gives birth to Inanna
(who does come back to life after this), or maybe to compassion;
or transformation itself. Maybe she was giving birth to the
integration of the light and the dark, as from this point in the
story both she and Inanna take on aspects of the other.

The deep mysteries of the Underworld, those that speak of
the transition between life and death, all involve ingesting
something. Why? There is the bread and the water of life in
Inanna's story; (echoed by the bread and the wine in Christ's last
supper); the pomegranate seeds in Persephone's story and in
Psyche's, the box of beauty ointment. In another Greek myth,

at of Orpheus, music is the thing ingested; his music which is so powerful that hearing it sways Persephone as Queen of the Underworld to relax her strict rules and release Orpheus' lover.

In symbolic thinking once we take something into ourselves it literally becomes part of us. This could be said to be true actually, as well as metaphorically. Think of medicines, of hallucinogenic or mind-altering substances, even of ordinary food. Let alone food as it exists in our current world, with debates over hormone-fed animals, fish dosed with antibiotics and genetically modified fruits, grains and vegetables. We are not separate from the things we ingest; their qualities are incorporated within us, in a not always quantifiable way. If it is something with mysterious qualities, those qualities are also understood to be transferred to us.

Thus Persephone, who ate seeds, becomes a seed herself, buried and reborn each year (generative). Psyche (who was already as beautiful as it was possible for a human being to be) after her ordeal attains a Goddess-level of beauty, as well as immortality. Inanna, on receiving the bread and water of life in the realm of death, gains the power to move between death and life, and with this she gains the power to decide who else will be sent to – and later rescued from – the Underworld. So the symbols these Goddesses are dealing with in the myth literally become the qualities they now embody. By interring these objects – ingesting them while they themselves are still 'buried' in the Underworld – they are assuming Underworld powers.

This same pattern occurs in Christ's story. At the Eucharist, worshippers ingest bread and wine that is thought – literally by some – to be his body and blood. In dying he has assumed the power to transmute death for others, a transformation which he passes on through this consumption of the Eucharist. Surely this is the same *bread of life and water of life,* as in the pre-dating Sumerian story. Christ himself becomes never-dying while at the same time retaining the symbol of always-dying, endlessly depicted on the cross. This is exactly the same as Osiris in earlier, Egyptian mythology, who was depicted as green to show himself as mummified (and regenerative).

The Underworld has the gates of both death and life within it. One can see this most clearly by Ereshkigal's actions; she kills Inanna and also gives life to her. Inanna, in her turn, is reborn from the Underworld but sends another there in her place, her consort Dumuzi. Psyche is gifted eternal life but the child she is carrying remains mortal, so that (immortal) life gives birth to life and death. Persephone gives birth to the seasons – to spring as she arises from the Underworld, and later to winter as she descends again; and thus the endless cycle. She has become the cycle of life itself but also, importantly, she is pregnant with new life – and therefore bound to the Underworld. Every child we give birth to is given over – even in that very act of birth – to eventual death. The child is born out of darkness and eventually returns there.

Down there, in the Underworld, one cannot stay polarized into a daylight self and a hidden self. They merge. One gives way to the other, just as the act of eating merges the substance – with all its magical meaning – with the one who eats. In the Underworld we lose our separation. All that we have denied, repressed and refrained from is let loose. We no longer have a 'good' self (whether it be a good mother, a good worker, a good dieter – whatever -) and a 'bad' self (the bad mother, the irresponsible worker, the slack dieter). We experience all aspects of ourselves, and out of that chaos something is resolved. Eventually a new version of our self is born. According to the basic pattern (of myth, dialectics and psychology) this new self is more whole, more deeply integrated and more integral to our true, or soul-self. At some point in the Underworld we stop holding our pain at a distance (Ereshkigal); we accept what is offered (Persephone); we give way to our curiosity and wanting more (Psyche). We accept what the Underworld has to offer, and

125

the grace of the Dark Goddess always involves transformation.

Grace is no longer particularly in vogue, perhaps because it cannot be bought, bargained for or relied on. It is a gift of the Gods. It is granted – sometimes – according to such factors as purity of heart, which one can never assess for oneself. When grace is present difficult things become possible; broken hearts are eased; a light is shone in the darkest places. One's efforts may be rewarded in the granting of grace but one cannot ensure it, rely on it or understand the form it will take, before it appears. It is of the divine and thus the mind behind it – if it is correct to call it mind – is unknowable to us. Possibly each instance of grace is unique, applicable only to that person in that moment.

When Psyche disobeys the instructions that until now have kept her safe and opens Persephone's box of beauty ointment, grace is attendant, because that is the action that leads to her being saved. It is with grace that the second half of Inanna's story runs so miraculously – she having done her best to stuff everything up, all the way through the first half. And it is surely grace that guides Persephone to eat those – was it five? seven? six? – pomegranate seeds, just before she is granted leave of the Underworld. These examples of grace may look like the exact opposite – destruction and an end to everything – yet without those exact destructions and ends, the new could not come forth. Grace cuts through difficulties, into the heart of things. It may well have two edges, like the two faces of the Dark Goddess; that of destruction as well as that of healing.

One way of understanding these mythic Underworld events as they play out in our personal, human lives is that we take our powerlessness into the Underworld and experience it totally. We take with us all of our loss, distress and helplessness and we are given as long as we need to wallow around in them. And, then, within the surrender (the ingesting) comes grace. There's a birth – of knowledge, power, self-determination, new life – and the task becomes one of integrating the qualities of each into the other (dark into light and light into dark; or death into birth and birth into death). The seed dies – and the tree is born. Kore dies and Persephone is born. Inanna and Ereshkigal 'die' as polarized opposites and incorporate aspects of the other into themselves. Psyche dies and becomes a Goddess. We die to our old selves and emerge, chrysalis-like, into the new.

When we return from our own Underworld journeys we have been changed by our encounter with the Dark Goddess and she is changed, as well. We have brought compassion to our own suffering (and it seems impossible to leave until we have done this). We have given new life to ourselves and these things have consequences; the actions have reactions that will play out in our lives. If, for example, in meeting with the Dark Goddess we have reclaimed the part of us that is an artist, when we return to the upper world that job as head accountant might have to go. If we have discovered our commitment to actively create social or political change, on returning we might decide that we will not have the large family we imagined, but instead limit ourselves to one, or no children. If we realized that what we yearned for was love and relationship we might have to leave that spiritual path dedicated to austerity and abstinence.

In visiting and revisiting the Dark Goddess there is no guarantee of what the outcome will be. Other people will also be affected, and may in turn carry out their own Underworld journeys. The only guarantee is that the results will have moved us at least a step further towards living the truth of our soul. And knowing that – instinctively, intuitively, having read the patterns or read the myths or followed the instructions or even unknow-ingly stumbled along a path of change and necessity – we have risked everything and given our selves and our lives over, to be remade. Remade – or reborn – by the Dark Goddess. Transformed in the cauldron of mysteries that is the Underworld. Alchemically altered in the crucible of our true self, another layer of dross burned off. Purified. Reborn.

Transformed.

INANNA IN THE UNDERWORLD

What happens when the main character is removed from the plot?

We all run a story that we are vital to the great plot of life. It is only ourselves holding things together; *without me no-one would eat in this house; the whole office would fall apart; the children would never get to school on time*... Yet another part of us knows full well that most of those things actually would happen if we weren't around, one way or another. In fact once we are removed the story goes on, often perfectly well.

Inanna is forcibly removed from her own plot in this section of her story. When she enters the Underworld, naked and bowed low she is greeted by Ereshkigal's Eye of Death. She is killed, straight away, with the Eye, with a scream, and with the realization of her own insignificance in that place. She's left hanging on a meat hook in the Underworld, dead. Yet events continue. Ereshkigal undergoes a transformation. From that implacable Goddess who recently ordered the gates of the Underworld to be locked, only to be opened one by one for her sister as her powers were stripped from her, she becomes helpless in enormous pain.

Ninshubur, meanwhile, having waited three days and nights is rushing around from city to city, temple to temple, carrying out Inanna's instructions for rescue. These instructions are discon- certingly far from fail-safe. The first two Gods – Inanna's grand- father and her own father – refuse to help. Jalaja Bonheim's inter- pretation on her CD, *The Descent of Inanna: A Guided Journey Through Ancient Sumerian Myth* has them sighing a little nostalgi- cally after Inanna's lost magnificence and saying, in effect, that she should have known better. Perhaps this is a way of showing that their powers are no longer equal to the situation; Inanna has already gone beyond them in authority and daring and now is in a different realm entirely. After all, no-one returns from the Underworld.

The third temple Ninshubur tries (and the last on the list) is that of Enki – Inanna's uncle and the God who created life. In order to rescue Inanna he makes two tiny creatures, the *galatur* and the *kurgarra*. Their names have no translation, they are unique beings. Inanna has gone beyond the known world and to be brought back, something entirely new needs to come into existence. Creativity, life-force and ingenuity are the ingredients needed for the first stage of this rescue. And persistence; Ninshubur has never despaired, hesitated or lost faith.

What does this tell us? Best to be prepared before you descend, for afterwards you may have no chance to help yourself. Best to leave clear instructions; best to have a number of back-up plans. Trying new things, that you have never done before, and persistence are keys to eventual release. And – finally – best to let go of any preference as to the outcome, for there is only a certain point up to which your actions can carry you. Past that, your fate is in the lap of the Gods.

The little creatures Enki makes are so tiny they can slip under the gates of the Underworld with no-one noticing. This is a clever trick and one worth considering for our own lives; what objects or ideas or feelings are so tiny, so unworthy of consider-ation that they can slip under the notice of everyday attention? A feeling so out of tune with normal life it has never been observed before? The kindness of a stranger? A line of music, suddenly singing straight at us? A prayer repeated again and again; a fresh flower placed daily on the altar? – maybe.

Enki gives one of the creatures a drop of the water of life and the other a crumb of the bread of life. He tells them Ereshkigal will be lying in agony and unattended on her bed. Instructing them in a simple form of compassion (a quality he has shown himself, in rescuing Inanna) he tells them to echo back Ereshkigal's complaints and griefs until she offers them a gift.

How did he know what would be happening down there? He can't have been there himself, for no-one ever returns from the Underworld. It must have been deduction; that peculiar circularity myths gather as they journey, so that past events predicate future ones – not exactly repeating them, but patterning them into meaning. And Enki is the God of Life, peculiarly relevant as what Ereshkigal is doing down there in the dark, on her own, appears to be giving birth. Perhaps Enki knew the balance must be kept. If Inanna was dead by her sister's hand, the death-sister would have to give birth.

The little fly-like beings successfully arrive in Ereshkigal's chamber. She is lying on a bed, unkempt and unattended, moaning and groaning. Each moan they echo, repeating her words. Each groan, each sigh they echo, letting her know someone is listening and that her pain is registered. To echo someone accurately you have to be in sympathy with them, you cannot do it callously or calculatedly. To truly echo back an expression of pain you have to feel it yourself, or the intonation of your voice would not convey the acknowledgement that exists in a genuine echoing. So they echo her and so they seem to feel *with* her.

This is a very tiny action but in Ereshkigal's chamber it is huge. No-one has given her this kind of attention before. She is astounded and offers them gifts, specifically *the water gift, the gift of grain,* and each gift they refuse. In the end she asks them what they do want. They ask for the corpse that is hanging on the hook. *You can't have that,* she tells them… but they persist and – like in a fairytale – now that she has offered them a gift their wish must be granted. Once the body is theirs (and obviously it had to be given to them, they couldn't just take it, or perform their little magical acts on it until it was theirs) they sprinkle the food of life and the water of life on it. Inanna's corpse comes back to life.

The food and water of life correspond exactly to the gifts Ereshkigal offered them previously; the gift of grain, the water gift. Obviously these gifts are extremely valuable in the Underworld; possibly even more potent than they are in the upper world, where we know they mean the difference between life and death. Even in death, apparently they still mythically create that difference, having the power to restore life to a corpse.

Inanna does not seem especially grateful to be rescued; she charges off back to the upper world and Ereshkigal is left alone, although there's no mention that she's in pain anymore. We are left to infer that the transformation has been a mutual one. Perhaps Inanna has been born again through Ereshkigal's labor, and this will be balanced by what is to come; Inanna's sweeping back up to her own realm attended by a flock of demons demanding another life in exchange for hers. In essence, she is carrying death with her. For the rules still stand; nobody can leave the Underworld. In this exceptional case where Inanna has left she must be replaced, so that one death will still be registered. The demons will not leave Inanna until they find her substitute.

MY OWN INANNA STORY: IN THE UNDERWORLD

In my literal enactment of the Inanna myth, at the Womens' Spirit Camp, I could not wait to go through those seven gates. I felt filled with energy and determination; focused on that moment of meeting Ereshkigal. The intervening first six gates were mere inconvenience.

When I crawled through Seventh Gate I was utterly prepared to meet her; I was looking forward to it. I was angry, determined. I knew exactly what I wanted to say, what I wanted to charge her with. I knew I had it in me to take her to task, to demand answers. It felt like the opportunity of a lifetime; here it is, the moment I can ask for justification. The reason for my life, the reason for suffering, the point of it all. I rose to my feet, my mouth opening to speak as I stared at Ereshkigal, shadowed on the throne. All of my eloquence deserted me but I still had some power in my lungs and the word *Why?* formed itself inside my head, as I began to breathe in and – still in that same first instant–

She turned and looked at me, pointed in the same motion and screamed.

The Eye of Death. The word of death. I recognized it. My body recognized it and dropped to the ground, not having spoken my question. I lay there, half-stunned until eventually two women came and dragged me to the side door. Some of my clothes were there – I had left them before I went through the gates. There was a fire outside, with a woman waiting. She offered warmth and a cup of tea which I did not want. I got dressed and went to bed.

The next day we did not speak but I was blank, filled with my knowledge that *you cannot even ask why.* There is no *why* – no question and no answer. You cannot ask the Dark Goddess *why* – she is her own why. Your questions – my questions – are less than the dust beneath her throne. She does not engage in dialogue, not even as uselessly as those gate keepers with their endless refrain which I obviously should have paid more attention to; *The ways of the Underworld are perfect. They may not be questioned.* May not be questioned indeed, literally. There is no way to question them.

This encounter with Ereshkigal left me deeply changed, in an almost wordless way. I think I embraced the mystery. I did not like it, at that stage, or understand it; but meeting it face to face like that, it was absolutely incontestable. This is one of the great truths, this exists. It is so. In effect, it may not be questioned. That is; you can question it all you like, but that will change nothing, affect nothing and questioning it is not the point. To be with it, to register what it is, to be a part of it, to see some part of it – that is enormous, magnificent and profound. It has no value, good or bad; it is neither other nor self. It is intrinsic. It is one of the mysteries.

THE UNDERWORLD IN OTHER MYTHS
Persephone
Imagining Persephone

I have heard that Persephone ate of the pomegranate whilst she was in the Underworld. Imagine her choosing that round fruit, weighing it in her hand before splitting it open; selecting the seeds with her fingertips and lifting them, one by one to her mouth. So deliberate. Those red seeds that stain the mouth like blood. It was that earth-blood in her that meant she could never leave the dark entirely, that she must always return. Do you see it as penance, for an error?

As I ate of the red pomegranate I knew that I was bonded to the earth and her fruits, not only in their bright life but also through the death in me. I am the witch and I will return, always, to my dark; beholden there by the blood fruit I recognized and tasted. You cannot keep away the killer, you cannot deny me. I celebrate the death within me on my return to the Underworld; I have interred the blood of the earth into my mouth and into my flesh and we are intrinsic now, each to the other. I am Persephone.

(Extract from 'Dancing the Red'; Jane Meredith.)

Did Persephone venture – or was she stolen – into the Underworld? These two interpretations of how she got there possibly say more about the culture viewing her activities than they do about Persephone. At one stage perhaps an audience could only believe she arrived in such an inhospitable 'dark' place by abduction. Surely nothing of her own will could lead her down there, to a place where she lost her maidenhood and her mother and vanished from the upper world? More recently, as women questioned this interpretation of events – maybe she just went exploring? Wanted more than an endless summer? Wanted to get away from her mother, or get into bed with Hades, or discover her own strengths? – it has seemed valid to suggest she was complicit in Hades' abduction of her, or even that she went on her own.

The nature of Persephone's time in the Underworld is not disclosed to us. Like Inanna she moves out of the central action of her own story, which is now carried by Demeter; as Ninshubur carries Inanna's story. Persephone is apparently in stasis all the time that Demeter roams the upper world searching for her daughter, not unlike a buried seed. We are told literally nothing about her except that – just before her rescue – Hades persuades her to eat the seeds of the pomegranate, and she becomes pregnant.

As a commentary to, and protest of her grief, Demeter has traveled across Greece, searching for news of her daughter. Even after she's been told where Persephone is, and that she can't get her back, she does not return to her duties of harvest and plenty; and so winter arrives for the first time upon the earth. Crops wither, animals starve and die, human communities (who of course are not prepared) are devastated and consequently their offerings to the Gods are diminished. Not only is this the advent of the first winter but there is no understanding that this new state of things will ever reverse. It is an apocalypse. When Zeus, king over all the Gods, finally realizes the extent of Demeter's powers and relents to Persephone's return he adds the caveat, *As long as she has eaten nothing while she was in the Underworld.*

The story as I read it implies it was only as Persephone was about to be released from the Underworld that she ate the seeds of the pomegranate and – it has long been understood – one cannot eat the food of the Underworld without binding oneself there. That's right; she went months without eating a thing and then suddenly, at the twelfth hour, she allowed herself to be tempted by a few pomegranate seeds. You would think the daughter of a Goddess would know better than this.

So why did she eat anything at all, let alone such suggestive objects as the glistening red seeds of the pomegranate? Because seeds, lest we forget, are exactly those things that – planted in the dark, their own Underworld of earth and winter – come to life again, creating a whole new plant quite magically. I can imagine Persephone holding out for a long time, refusing to eat anything; whether out of perversity, fear, or keeping her options open. While she does not eat the food, she remains still of the upper world. Yet as news of her – conditional – release comes wafting down the corridors of the Underworld, suddenly she eats something. *What is this?* – as Inanna might ask.

I think it is Persephone's very calculated and precise bid to retain the powers of the Underworld, without entirely sacrificing her place in the upper world. In other words she has discovered her rightful domain. Down there she is Queen of the Underworld, whereas in the meadows and fields she was only Demeter's daughter. And in becoming pregnant to Hades she is signaling her feminine, regenerative power; to rebirth the souls in the Underworld.

Not tasting the pomegranate until the last minute is what any of us might do, upon visiting our own darkness. At first we may imagine it is an awful place; we may believe we have been abducted; we cannot escape and we refuse to have anything to do with the foods and riches there. Then (eventually) seeing the light in the distance and the possibility of return, we seek to retain the self and powers we have suddenly discovered are part of the Underworld. We wish to keep them with us as we return to our upper world life. It is what Inanna does, trailing demons as she arises to set her world justly back to rights. It is what Psyche does, opening Persephone's box of beauty ointment as she travels the paths back to the upper world. It is a bid for integration.

So what happened to Persephone, exactly? She ate something; she had sex; she became pregnant; she became a Queen. These things are all related. Shrouded in the mystery of the Underworld and those hidden months, still the emblems stand out starkly. Eating, sex, conception, power. Food (ingesting life), sex (a different ingestion), conception (creating life) and power –

in Persephone's case, power within the realm of death. A power of the living over the dead. Everything Persephone does down there has to do with life. She has gone into the darkest place and brought new life, a gift of regeneration she perhaps inherited from her mother. She has ingested seeds, she has even made the remote Hades into a lover, husband and father-to-be. And on her return to the upper world, because of Demeter's joy at the return of her daughter, Persephone brings – or more literally is – the spring that arrives when the earth is in the grip of winter.

Persephone has gone into the darkest place and dealt in life. She has twisted two versions of herself together – innocent, daylight maiden and dark, fertile queen. Comparing myths, she has taken Inanna and Ereshkigal's roles and held them both. Coming and going from the Underworld as she does each year she reinforces her dual nature. Inanna and Ereshkigal have one climactic confrontation that changes everything forever but Persephone quietly goes about her business, shuttling between living (conceiving in the dark, arising as spring on the earth) and dying (the creator of every winter as she descends again; the Queen of death herself).

Psyche

When we meet Persephone in Psyche's story, as Queen of the Underworld, she kindly grants Psyche's request for the box of beauty ointment, perhaps knowing her gift will not reach its intended destination – or perhaps it already has? Perhaps, together with Aphrodite, she is playing a subtler hand, knowing that no mortal woman will be able to resist opening this box only meant for Goddesses? Perhaps, even, she is helping Psyche fulfill her quest the only way it can be fulfilled, by transcending both life and death?

Again it is a transition far from guaranteed. It relies on Psyche obeying all her instructions meticulously – and then disobeying this last instruction. Not disobeying it right away; she has to get out of Persephone's presence, back past the three-headed guard dog (with the second piece of her bread) back over the river (with her second coin to pay the ferryman) and into the winding underground paths before she disobeys. But if – if – she does all that, then the myth can come to fruition.

In opening the box Psyche lets forth the deadly substance Aphrodite has requested. She is overcome and falls dead to the ground. Luckily this motivates Eros, her lost lover, as nothing else has done since the start of her travails. Perhaps he had been fine watching her suffer and toil and grieve, but her death was too much to bear? Perhaps, perhaps even, those greater, wiser, more far-seeing than he stayed his hand until the fatal moment? Looked at this way it could well be that Aphrodite is not set against the lovers but rather assisting them, ensuring the only set of actions that will result in their eventual, and eternal, reunion.

This brings to mind a further Greek myth, that of Pandora, whose opening of 'the box' (apparently long mis-translated and actually a pithos, those huge and beautiful Mediterranean clay pots, in which olive oil and other perishables were stored) releases all the ills of the world, as well as hope. The slang meaning of 'box' in English is more than a little ironic (she opened her vulva? her vagina?) and actually doubles the imagery of those pithoi, some of which are as tall as a woman and shaped provocatively with a pregnant belly, containing precious things.

The links between death and what emerges from women's boxes is not casual or happenstance. We see it in Inanna's story, (she is reborn); in Persephone's and also in Psyche's; both of these last are pregnant, as well as being reborn (Psyche) into immortality and bringing rebirth to the whole earth (Persephone). As for *all the ills of the world, and hope* – or in other versions, simply *everything* – what can one say? That's where we all come from, out of women. There are overtones of this rebirth through women in Christ's story; where he emerges from a cave (the dark earth) after interment and appears to Mary Magdalene. The Egyptian story of Osiris contains this theme as well. He was interred in a sarcophagus, then later cut into pieces and scattered, finally to be reassembled by his sister-wife Isis. She made love with him (although he was still technically dead) and conceived their son.

Stepping into the unknown is an essential of the Underworld. You can trust in the process itself, but you can hardly trust the outcome, since you cannot know it. The risks taken in these stories are immense; these Goddesses gamble with everything. For us mortal women, our Underworld journeys feel just as immense, frightening and uncertain. Our only surety is that by following in the footsteps of Inanna, of Persephone, of Psyche we can embody their learning; that rebirth and integration are won this way; by entering the unknown and accepting, even ingesting what we find there.

RITUAL: LISTENING TO THE DARK GODDESS

The intention of this ritual is to listen to the Dark Goddess in the Underworld.

Time: 1 hour

You will need:

- Pillows or cushions (and a blanket if you think you will get cold)
- Your journal or paper and pen. Coloring things are optional
- Your altar, or at least a candle
- Read through the whole ritual before beginning

Preparation

This is a deep inner ritual. You may feel an hour is a long time to be quiet and go within. But part of the Underworld experience is waiting; it is a powerful element of both Inanna and Persephone's myths. In Inanna's story listening to the Dark Goddess provides crucial turning points of the myth; both when Inanna, above ground, hears her sister calling from below and then in the Underworld, when Inanna's tiny rescuers practice active listening. In our own, real life experiences of the Underworld we are often impelled into inaction, experiencing an inarguable time of nothingness, blankness and helplessness as we await further developments or understandings. During this time we can hear little of the outer world. We are waiting to learn to hear again our own voice, speaking from within.

Create a womb-like environment for this ritual, although preferably not in your bed. Setting up pillows, cushions and maybe a blanket near your altar is perfect. Keep the lights dim (or off) and light a single candle on your altar. If you prefer, you can do this ritual completely in the dark. Do not have music playing, and eliminate outside noise as best you can. If you live somewhere with loud traffic or industrial noise it is best to do this ritual at a very quiet time of day; early in the morning or late at night.

You may find it helpful to do this ritual at a special time anyway, such as midnight on a dark moon; or in a special place such as a temple, meditation space or outside on land that is sacred to you. Like other rituals and processes it is best to ensure you will not be distracted, interrupted or called away, so take some practical measures to ensure this. Unplug or turn off the phone. Wait until you have the house to yourself, or make very clear arrangements with the other people there (even if some of them are your children) that you are not to be interrupted. If you are going to do the ritual outside, make sure you have taken sensible safety precautions.

The Ritual

- Begin by cleansing your space; rearranging (or creating) your altar; casting a circle or doing whatever you prefer to prepare yourself for ritual.

- When you are ready light your candle and sit in front of it. You may already experience a strong sense of being within the Underworld, due to progressing through this book and the rituals here, or through circumstances in your own life. If not, it is now your task to take yourself there. Remember to leave a part of yourself (your conscious awareness) 'outside' the gates to the Underworld, as you journey downwards and within.

- You may choose to use meditation to take yourself down and within; or if you prefer you can think slowly through Inanna's story and the seven gates she descended through. Otherwise you can simply concentrate on envisaging and experiencing as fully as you can a sense of the Underworld around you. Take some time, even as much as twenty minutes. Close your eyes if you like.

- When you feel either that you are fully in the Underworld, or that you cannot get much deeper at this time, lie down and place your ear to the ground (or to a cushion). Now listen.

You may hear your own breath and heartbeat. Listen to these for a while and then listen more deeply. Go more deeply down than you did with the *Placing Your Ear to the Ground* ritual. Listen with your innermost soul.

Listen. Even if you hear nothing, or nothing much, keep listening. Imagine opening your ear, within realms we are not usually aware of. You may hear whispers, sighs, cries, screams or words or nothing at all. No matter what you hear, this is just a period of listening, you do not have to respond. Think of Inanna, hanging dead on a meat hook while Ereshkigal cried and moaned. Inanna did not have to do anything about those cries and screams, right then.

Can you hear a voice? It might be your own voice, or the voice of the Goddess, or the voice of the earth itself. You might find yourself breathing out words that seem to come from somewhere beyond you, or feel the need to speak yourself. Speak if you want to, but remember this is primarily a listening ritual, so listen closely to anything that comes out of your mouth. You may hear voices inside your own head; listen to these, as well.

After listening for a while – at least fifteen minutes but maybe for up to half an hour – bring yourself back to a sitting position, and orient yourself back to your surroundings. Sit for a few minutes in stillness, watching the candle flame again or concentrating on your breathing. Then raise the lighting, or turn on a lamp so you can record your ritual in your journal.

Even if you heard nothing at all, record your own feelings and reactions, whether they be frustration, fear, boredom, anger, peace, distress or any other feelings. These feelings and reactions can tell you a lot about your relationship with the Dark Goddess and the Underworld. Recording what you heard and felt is taking the part of the *kurgarra* and the *galatur*, letting Ereshkigal know someone is listening. It was this simple act that led to Inanna's release. When we hear the Dark Goddess we begin to release the world from its stagnation of refusing the dark. If we learn to hear ourselves in our own pain and suffering it can lead to release from our own dark places, where we are struggling to give birth to the new.

As well as writing (or instead) you can do a drawing that records something of what you felt or heard. You also might like to 'free write' a passage of the Dark Goddess speaking. To do this, imagine you *are* the Dark Goddess, living in the Underworld, and write in the first person. Write without editing in your mind, or on the page, what comes to you. Your writing may be raw, messy, ungrammatical or hesitant. You can set yourself a goal (one entire page of writing, or five minutes of writing) if you feel uncertain about this process, and then stop when you have reached the goal. Read back what you wrote.

It might be that you hear or think about the state of the world, rather than your personal issues when you listen to the Dark Goddess. This is valid, and you can record what you heard or thought. However, also ask yourself if there is a special message to you, either within this information or another message. Sometimes general messages can include very specific ones. For example if you hear a message about the neglect of the earth it is advisable to ask yourself if you are neglecting yourself; or if you feel neglected by others. This is not to invalidate the original message, but adds to understanding why you might be hearing it at this time. Similarly, you will not be able to solve the neglect of the earth by changing your own situation so that you don't feel neglected; but on the other hand, perhaps you won't be effective in reversing the neglect of the earth until you, yourself, have resolved your feelings or personal experience of neglect.

You may wish to repeat the ritual of Listening to the Dark Goddess, or even practice it regularly, for example each Winter Solstice or at the dark of each moon. It is a crucial practice if we wish to learn how to balance out the light and dark in our lives and in the world.

A SAMPLE DESCENT: IN THE UNDERWORLD

A long time after I went through those seven gates, giving everything up I rise from the floor. I feel cleansed. I feel ghost-like. I could dress and walk out of this house and disappear from my former life. I feel absolutely in possession of my senses and unrelated to all possible outcomes. My wedding ring still lies in the chalice on the altar. I do not glance at it. My path lies elsewhere.

Down here I heard Ereshkigal's sobbing; her screaming, gasping and coughing and I felt it as close to my heart as could be, since it was mine. My love and sympathy flow towards her. *Oh, what a mess you have got yourself into. Never mind; never mind, love; all can be undone. You are the one who undoes everything.* Here is the compassion of the Dark Goddess.

Now that I am clear of all those possessions of Inanna's; all those aspects of my life, I am able to begin the work. I decide to tackle the seven gates, to remake those seven sections of my life. I'm not really thinking properly, because probably I should have stayed down there for three days, following the map of the myth, but I am impatient and begin work straight away. I decide to take seven actions, to balance the gates, and these actions will be things I have not done before. They will break the old patterns I gave away as I descended.

In two ways beginning this work straight away makes no difference. Firstly, I was confused enough to try to go back through the gates in the wrong order – I began again at the First Gate, without realizing that of course Ascents begin at the Seventh Gate. Secondly, at the end of the day I did not pick up my wedding ring and put it on again. I wondered what would happen, when my partner asked where it was. I decided to say, *It is in the chalice on the altar.* Actually, he didn't notice I wasn't wearing it. I left it there for three days, waiting for something to happen and in the end what happened was I had to go and pick up another ring, that was being resized. I put all my rings on, and on my way out the door grabbed that one from the chalice, just so I didn't have one bare finger, and put it on again. Happenstance. It was just a ring, now, one I wore on the ring finger of my left hand.

Six months later, in spring, I looked at that ring on my finger and wondered where the specialness had gone. *Oh; I cast it out, back when I did that Descent. Oh yes. I remember. It became ordinary for me, it lost its promise.* Missing it, I weep. *Do I want it back, that potential, that magic encoded in the alchemy of silver-and-gold that I wear since my wedding ceremony? Oh yes, I think I do.* That's when I realize I never did a proper Ascent; that I have been down here in the Underworld all that time.

And yes, I stayed there six months. I thought I did it in one day – a three hour Descent, not bad. Not bad at all, but really it took six months to emerge from that little sojourn with my beloved sister, the Dark Goddess, and perhaps I was healed in that time; protected, anyway.

One thing I did during that six months was complete a whole book of someone else's process; *The Mythic Path* by David Feinstein and Stanley Krippner, appropriately subtitled *Discovering the Guiding Stories of Your Past – Creating a Vision for Your Future*. Following this program involved creating (or realizing) my own personal guiding mythology and working with it in various ways. Towards the end of the book I had to find a way to symbolize the changes I had made internally, to my guiding mythos. I fixed it all into a Beltaine ritual for about twenty people that embodied bringing my inner, private self out into the world. Perfect timing; coming up from the Underworld with Persephone in spring.

Dream

I was outside in the dark, alone on a moor that seemed to stretch in all directions, darkly and unevenly and uneventfully. I was wandering around, lost and not even knowing what I was looking for. After a long while I saw a small light in the distance, moving towards me. I waited and as it came closer I could see there were three women, huddled together, the centre one bent over by age and holding a lantern. The women on either side of her were younger and she leaned on their arms, they were supporting her. I saw them as priestesses; acolytes; the triple Goddess.

When they reached me I saw the old woman was a teacher I'd had, long ago; a remarkable woman of vibrant spirit, intellect and ferocity who had displayed warmth and humor in spite of great physical pain. Even alive she had been bent over, hands slightly clawed but that had not stopped her teaching full time or treating her students to her blend of incisive clarity, startlingly high expectations and genuine support. She died only a year or two after she taught me, she had not been especially old and I felt her loss as an abrupt lessening in the world.

In the dream she looked me in the eye and I was startled by her presence, her obvious life and my confusion at meeting her in this dark wasteland. *I had forgotten you*, I said and it was in wonder, that she had arrived out of nowhere when I thought she was dead. She looked at me closely, dryly but with a spark in her eye and a lift in the corners of her mouth. *We never forgot you*, she said and as she spoke the words, I knew it as the truth.

WHAT TO DO IN THE UNDERWORLD

There are many processes you can use to assist you while you are in the Underworld. Three that I particularly like are outlined below. I think of them all as short cuts. It's also good to recognize when your time in the Underworld is up, and for that, recognition of the turning point is vital. Many of us try to race to that turning point, without doing much work on the way. If you feel a strong – even irresistible – urge to skip over these next three processes to get to the turning point, this is a warning sign. It's your self-protection, leaping in to save what you left behind at the seven gates. Probably your level of resistance to these processes is in direct proportion to their potential usefulness.

Getting at the Truth

With thanks to Byron Katie for her Work.

Truth can be elusive. Often we think and believe we have scraped the bottom of our souls to come up with the truth – and we have. It's just that so much more remains hidden to us. There are techniques around to help you discover these hidden truths. They are not comfortable, although once I force myself to do them I usually experience great relief and understanding.

The simplest method I know is a very abbreviated version of a process I was taught as part of the Byron Katie process. Byron

Katie herself has written extensively about The Work of questioning and turning around fears and assumptions that we carry around with us, and there are teachers and workshops that detail it in depth. I recommend it. This process of getting at the truth is a quick way of undercutting your own stories about what's going on and bringing them home to the originator of the stories; you. It's quite ruthless. It's also efficient, simple and incontestable.

This is best done as a writing exercise. There are three steps, as I do it.

At Step One you choose a situation about which you are unhappy. It could be a relationship; a workplace situation; a family dynamic. The important thing is that it is something other people are involved with, not solely an internal-to-you matter. You then write, freehand and as fast as possible everything that makes you unhappy with that situation, concentrating on the other people involved. List exactly what they are doing and why you don't like it. You can use their names or just pronouns; 'he', 'she' or 'they'. Write as much as you can, detailing your complaints thoroughly. Let loose. Do not worry what someone else would think if they were to read this or know you think like this, no-one else is going to read it and in the next few steps it will become completely transformed. Write until there is nothing more to say about the situation.

Step Two involves you re-writing the entire passage you just wrote. Each time you get to someone else's name, or the pronouns 'he', 'she' or 'they' you replace it with the word 'I', 'I'm', 'me' or 'myself'. Do not stop at this stage to ponder on meaning, just re-write the whole thing, making those changes. (You might have to make a few grammatical changes as well; such as changing *she always does* to *I always do*.)

At Step Three you read back through what you've written. Read the first piece of writing. Then read the second piece of writing, slowly and preferably aloud. Pause as you read, to let the words sink in. Some sentences will not mean much, anymore, but some will be piercing in their relevance. Piercing, as in a light shining in the dark. The meanings will turn around and evolve, uncovering strange betrayals of the self, hidden 'shadow' aspects of your personality and also, miraculously, a way forward in this situation you've been unhappy with. Basically you have now revealed (some of) your projections.

Of course this is only one part of the truth you have uncovered – but it is a part of your own truth, and a part you can do something about. What I do after reading it through once is go back and read it through again (still slowly) and this time underline, or circle the sentences or part-sentences that mean the most to me. Then I rewrite these out again, underneath, and accept them as part of my truth that has remained hidden until now, disguised in my feelings about another's behavior. Here is a (short) example of my own.

Step One: *I can't bear it that he keeps reacting. That everything I say or do he relates to himself. That he's so negative, all the time. He over-reacts, he's so protective and defensive all the time he can't hear anything I'm saying. He doesn't know who I am. He seems to want me to be different. He doesn't like my answers – my truth – he's offended and hurt by the simplest things. He wants too much from me. Too much time and attention. He's too emotional for me – I think he's into drama. That covers up his perceived inadequacy.*

Step Two: *I can't bear it that I keep reacting. That everything I say or do, I relate to myself. That I'm so negative, all the time. I over-react – I'm so protective and defensive all the time I can't hear anything I'm saying. I don't know who I am. I seem to want me to be different. I don't like my answers – my truth – I'm offended and hurt by the simplest things. I want too much from myself. Too much time and attention. I'm too emotional for myself – I think I'm into drama. That covers up my perceived inadequacy.*

Step Three: *I can't bear it that I keep reacting. That everything I say or do, I relate to myself. That I'm so negative, all the time. I over-react – I'm so protective and defensive all the time I can't hear anything I'm saying. I don't know who I am. I seem to want me to be different. I don't like my answers – my truth – I'm offended and hurt by the simplest things. I want too much from myself. Too much time and attention. I'm too emotional for myself – I think I'm into drama. That covers up my perceived inadequacy.*

Conclusions: **I can't bear it that I keep reacting. I over-react. I can't hear anything I'm saying. I don't know who I am. I don't like my answers – my truth. I want too much from myself.**

Once you have these statements of deep truth you can begin to address them. In the example above, I firstly have to learn not to react so much. I think of myself as a person who *doesn't* react, so obviously I am covering it up really well. But that doesn't mean I'm not reacting. When I read that sentence in the first person it shot home with a dreadful, sad ring of truth. I don't want to be reactive, that's why I cover it up so fiercely. But truly, inside myself, I do react, again and again. I would like for the cover story (that I'm not a very reactive person) to be real; so I will probably do the work that's been pointed to by this truth-telling and start unpicking my reactiveness.

Some of the deeper statements, *I don't know who I am* and *I want too much from myself* I will have to sit with for a while. I can understand them, in this particular context, and forgive them, though I feel sad about them. They will lead me to re-evaluate how I am acting in this relationship, whether what I am putting into it is genuine, or more of a reflection of what I think the expectations are. Hopefully I will be able to change this piece by piece, to come more from myself and so remember who I am, both in and out of the relationship.

Lastly the statement *I don't like my answers – my truth* – seems a summation of this process. No, I don't like them; but there they are and here I am. Actually, it's okay. I don't like it but I can deal; which is a step ahead than I was before I began this process.

As a final step I like to read back through my original piece of writing. If the process is working this will have faded in power as a result of undertaking the other steps. That is, those sentiments are finding their rightful place.

Secondary Gains and Taking 100% Responsibility

Secondary gains are very tricky things and well worth taking a look at. A secondary gain is something you receive from a situation, which – even if the situation appears to be quite negative – actually suits you (or some might prefer to say, it suits a shadow part of you). It is hidden under other, more obvious gains or losses. Secondary gains are not usually the sorts of things one would confess to. But while they remain unacknowledged it can be impossible to create change. Only by dragging secondary gains out into the harsh light of day – or maybe the dim, comforting surrounds of the Underworld, where nothing appears to make too much impact – can we unhook them from sending their small, steady stream of energy into a situation we are wrestling with.

To get at secondary gains we have to look firstly at primary gains. Primary gains are fairly obvious. For example, *By sending my child to school I am ensuring her education is taken care of.* The secondary gain, which lies underneath the primary gain (not so obvious, not such a big player, but still there); is perhaps something like; *By sending my child to school I get my life back.* A primary gain is usually the obvious, most straight-forward reason we have for an action or behavior of our own; the secondary gain/s (and there can certainly be more than one) kind of tick away underneath. They may appear unworthy (that is, you wouldn't like to admit to them) or even outright destructive. For example; *In failing to find a job my primary gain is that I retain my freedom.* My secondary gain might be that *I never have to discover if I can hold down a job or not.*

You can practice on positive life situations. For example the primary gain of eating healthy food is *to keep my body healthy.* The secondary gain may be something less attractive; *so people will think I am pure,* for instance. A primary gain of being generous with money may be the pleasure you wish to bring people, and that you receive yourself from being generous. A secondary gain may be to keep people happy; to cover up your selfishness or to differentiate yourself from a miserly parent, partner or other role-model. A primary gain of getting married could be to make a commitment to the person you love; whereas a secondary gain could be to ensure you won't be alone, or to have a built-in companion/lover/economic support. In complex scenarios like this there can be many secondary gains.

But the real goal is to begin to focus on difficult, troublesome or disastrous life situations. Here, even the primary gain can be very awkward or painful to acknowledge. This is partly because none of them look pretty but also because it involves taking responsibility. It's one thing to take responsibility for things we have happily chosen for ourselves (starting a new relationship, taking a course we have longed to do, joining an interest group); it's debatable to take responsibility for things we have less choice in (staying in a particular job, missing out on being a parent, maintaining working relationships with those around us). What about situations we have had no choice at all in – or at least we feel that way – experiencing a debilitating illness, losing a job or being rejected in love?

There's an interesting trick which I find useful (it's a short cut). Forget the rights and wrongs of the whole thing, just for the purpose of this exercise. They'll still be there at the end, but by then you'll have more insight into your sub-conscious operations. Imagine, just for a moment, that you DO have one hundred percent responsibility for everything that happens in your life.

Some people might think of this as karma, that they are paying off debts and bringing balance to situations from a previous lifetime (or even the current lifetime). Others might see it as a way of bringing power and choice back into your life; and still others might see it as a 'god-self', giving exactly the right lessons and experiences at every moment.

However you see it try to imagine for a moment that you are one hundred percent responsible for everything that's happening to you. Let's examine a relationship problem. Usually, blame is assumed to be about fifty-fifty. There's two sides to every dispute, it takes two to argue... More often in our minds, we load sixty, eighty, ninety or even one hundred percent of blame onto the other person. *It's because he won't communicate; She's jealous because she's insecure; She's only interested in the kids; He had a terrible childhood; She doesn't know how to commit; He's too demanding...* Even if we are guilty of this, we can still look at primary and secondary gains. A primary gain of being with someone who won't commit might be fairly clear; we don't have to commit ourselves. The secondary gain may be something like, we won't have to admit this is the wrong relationship for us; or, it leaves us free to continue all the behaviors our lover doesn't like. Obviously these are not comfortable truths, but this is what is assisting us, with a little self-excusing, to stay right in that relationship and go right on complaining that the other person just won't commit.

When you – even momentarily – become one hundred percent responsible for the situation it becomes far less comfortable to stay in it. In other words, the one hundred percent responsibility is an agent for change. If I am one hundred percent responsible for this (uncommitted) relationship – that means I CHOSE this in the first place and I CONTINUE TO CHOOSE IT. Many rational arguments can be brought against this – I didn't know this person couldn't or wouldn't commit when we got together; people change; I'm only part or half of the equation... etcetera.

JOURNEY TO THE DARK GODDESS

That is not useful, and certainly not the short cut. Instead, imagine what it means, to be one hundred percent responsible. Very simply, it means I am choosing to be in an uncommitted relationship. Is that what I want? By the very fact of my complaining about the other person's lack of commitment, I'm saying it's not.

Follow this with some moments of truth. I may discover it IS what I want, after all; I don't want to commit, myself. Perhaps that was just an old record I picked up from my parents, or from everyone else around me settling down... In which case I now know myself better and can drop that complaint and get on with my life and the relationship as it is. If this happens to you, notice if something else replaces the 'she/he can't commit' complaint – it may have been a cover-up for a deeper dissatisfaction. You can then apply these processes to that deeper issue.

If you are spending time in the Underworld, however, chances are you will discover that it's not what you want. That you want – in this instance – commitment in a relationship. Only when you take responsibility for NOT being in a committed relationship (*I chose this, this is my choice, this is the relationship I have chosen to be in and am still in*) can you begin to really change what is happening outside of yourself. You may discover, when you ask yourself honestly if you would be willing and able to commit to this relationship, that the answer is no. Or you may find the answer is yes; but if the other person, when asked seriously to consider it, still gives you a no, you are faced with a dilemma. In the upper world these things are not necessarily such great dilemmas; one accepts the answer and either stays in an unsatisfactory relationship, or leaves it. Or one denies the answer, hanging on and waiting for the other person to change, although we rarely believe we will change ourselves.

But in the Underworld these things may be accepted only after great inner battle. Death, in fact. Death of your hopes for this relationship, of your understanding of your own motivations in relationship, of your ability in life – so far – to create or find what you want. This is because you are usually dealing with not just a single instance – whether it be a relationship, an illness, depression or other difficulty – but a pattern, and often a whole lifetime's pattern. Sometimes it is even a generational pattern. In the Underworld you have to change not just on the surface level – this instance of the event – but all the way through, down to the core. In the Underworld you get to rewrite your own pattern. This can take a while. It can look messy. It is usually deeply distressing, revelatory and freeing.

It's well-known that emotions take a while to change. They tend to catch up to behaviors, rather than behavioral change being the *result* of emotional change. As anyone knows who's successfully started an exercise regime, made constructive changes in communication styles or learnt a new language, this works; better than you might expect and with much less angst than anticipated. So with these processes – owning up to secondary gains and taking one hundred percent responsibility – I don't advocate waiting until it feels comfortable or sits right. It's going to sit all wrong, ruffle your fur backwards and make you feel like throwing up – at the very least. But it will get results.

When you find yourself up against outside events – a death, a natural disaster, someone else's attitude to you – it would be cruel and unnecessary to try to take responsibility for these events. Obviously (most of the time) I didn't cause them, I can't *actually* take one hundred percent responsibility for them. But I can always take one hundred percent responsibility for the way I am dealing with them. It's been said in a variety of ways; the only person you can change is yourself; the only change you can effect is inside your own mind and the choice you always have is how you look at something. Taking one hundred percent responsibility for *that*, and understanding the secondary gains of the way you have chosen to deal with these life crises can move you a whole lot further on, through the Underworld and towards your Ascent.

Speaking with the Voice of the Dark Goddess

Giving Ereshkigal a voice to speak with, to sigh and scream and sob and moan and groan with is a valuable and cathartic process. Sometimes this voice just bursts out of us, as we erupt in anger, grief or distress. Often it's accompanied by a sense of horror or embarrassment as we realize it is us making that noise and although it can be a relief to have got all that stuff out, it also can be inappropriate, misdirected and hurtful; even – potentially – abusive.

When we willingly give the Dark Goddess a voice she is less likely to explode in an unpredictable way. This means we can choose either who should hear this voice (and I would only advise a very close friend, a support or ritual group or a counselor) or to be completely alone when we give voice to her. I am not talking here about the faint-cries-from-far-away, this is the full-on screaming and echoing back stuff that happens deep in the Underworld.

The need to speak – or yell or scream – out from the Underworld may just come upon you. Or you may spend a lot of time determinedly repressing this voice and so have ready access to it, once you give it permission. Or you may have to encourage this voice, or even force it out, employing that old trick of *fake it til you make it*. Creating space for the voice of the Dark Goddess to come out of you, for what needs to be spoken or – mythically speaking – for Ereshkigal's moaning and groaning to emerge will assist your progression through the Underworld. Even at the times when you may feel nothing at all is happening, that you are literally hanging on the meat hook dead to your own life, undertaking such activities will be moving your story along to the next stage.

You may end up giving a seemly, quiet and ladylike expression to the voice of Ereshkigal. Or not. It's hard to know, before it starts happening. So the best thing is to plan for it to be loud.

There are a variety of ways to do this without drawing too much attention to yourself. Some women swear by screaming when they're alone in the car. It's true, no-one outside the car can hear it; but I worry about the safety aspect. Invoking the Dark Goddess while you're driving seems inherently dangerous. Other women tell me they do it in the shower, but unlike the car, people can quite easily hear you, unless you are just moderately sobbing, in which case the extravagance and freedom has gone out of it. Another way I've experimented with – and I don't like it, but it may be your only alternative – is to scream into a pillow or cushion. This does muffle the sound almost entirely, no matter how hard or loud you scream, but breathing is impossible, and co-coordinating between breathing and screaming can be limiting (or just tricky and distracting).

The two most satisfactory methods I have found are in a sound proof room (amazingly, some counselors do have these, as well as music studios, for instance) or – best of all – at the beach next to a crashing surf. This is particularly good because it's outside, in a beautiful, natural environment (though I suppose an underground room could seem even more appropriate) and because it is at the beach, you can see a long way in either direction and check that no-one is nearby. Cliff tops or waterfalls could provide the same benefits.

I've given voice to the Dark Goddess in all of these situations. Sometimes she just rips through and is done; other times there is a longish period of slowly rising energy. One way to get yourself into the expression of it, if you're not there already, is through keening; that high, almost continuous wailing that is associated with women in mourning. Especially combined with squatting, and rocking backwards and forwards, this is a very powerful way of opening a channel directly into hidden or with-held pain and grief. I've done this several times with groups of women –

keening and allowing anything else to break through – and it creates a shared wordless place; the connection of the Dark Goddess.

You may be someone who freely voices her concerns and emotions and doesn't mind a bit of rage. Or not. For those of us who are quieter, or by preference stifle some of our full expression, this exercise of giving voice to the Dark Goddess is a powerful teaching. It is one of those things where the stronger your resistance is to it, the more you would be well advised to do it. If what comes out of your mouth is not just screams and cries, but actual words, understandings or directives, make sure you record them afterwards, so you can work with them later.

Recognizing the Turning Point

There is usually a huge relief that accompanies being in the Underworld, when we have done a thorough Descent. It is impossible to explain this properly before it happens. All that trauma, relinquishing everything at gate after gate and then – how can there be peace? How stillness? How serenity? Everything else has run out, been used up, paid as a price to enter this place and there is nothing left. In a Persephone workshop I ran recently almost all the participants found themselves, after the Descent, in a place of wonder and peace. Stillness, some described it as, or emptiness. At first the emptiness was confronting, alarming to those who had been used to a life full of constant demands, activities and necessity. To find – nothing – was disturbing. Yet by the following day the woman who felt this most devastatingly was embracing it, reluctant even to Ascend lest she lose this feeling of emptiness she was suddenly treasuring.

One woman startled into the realization that all her struggle and pain of years was part the Descent, of the letting go of precious things; yet once she did that (even in ritual), she experienced a deep peace that she had never got to in her real-life experience of struggling to hold onto things. Another woman spoke of a dark, wide river; swimming there amongst a thousand souls she did not know, of the utter rightness and belonging of it. Listening to her I was reminded of the Underworld river Styx; the souls of the dead waiting to be reborn; of sperm swimming up fallopian tubes and babies being born in a rush of waters.

There are different types of turning points. There's vivid in-the-moment turning points; historic understanding-one's-past-journey turning points; and archetypal turning points echoing the myths and stories of Descent. Another of the Persephone workshop women spoke of her great reluctance to 'stay down' – that as soon as she touched the depths of the Underworld, she struggled to be free and so never fully experienced the natural conclusions of the process. To her, the feeling of peace was so unfamiliar it was alarming. This artificial turning point, where you have forced it through, may be common but is not in keeping with a conscious Descent. We are interested not in *creating* a turning point, but in *recognizing* it.

How do you recognize the turning point, if you are in the Underworld? That moment when you are rescued from doom, from the meat hook, the stillness, the nothingness, the uncertainty? How will you know when things turn around and it stops being a Descent story and starts to be about Ascent?

You will be offered the bread of life and the water of life. Not just offered it; it will be sprinkled upon you. You will not be able to refuse it. If you are following the story, the map laid down in ancient myth, you will arise then and begin your Ascent, step by step.

What is the bread of life, the water of life? It may come to each woman differently, and to each woman a different way each time. These central mysteries are symbols. Thus we can say; *the bread of life and the water of life are what enable Inanna to arise.* Nowhere does it explain what these things are, but in my reading of the story it seems as simple as; they are bread and water. Bread and water from the land of the living. Something that has got through the vast distance between the upper world and the Underworld and has reached Inanna. There were agents to bring it to her and those agents were set in motion by her own, earlier, decree. That is important, but at this stage of the story it is not the main point. The main point is that they reach her and they have an animating effect.

The bread and the water of life may be the voices of your children that you hear, through your depression. I have known them, for one woman, to be the knowledge – not the trivial knowledge, that everyone knows this thing, but the deep, body-lived Goddess-arising, this is the heart of the mystery knowledge – that spring comes after winter. For one woman, who told me with tears running down her face that her heart had turned to ice, it came when I offered her a piece of my own heart. I have many times seen the bread and water of life be simple acceptance by others of one's truth. Sometimes the truth is tragic or horrific; the molestation of her daughter by her husband was one woman's truth. Another woman's story, of extreme sensitivity to the modern world and her debilitating allergies and illness may seem simple to us in comparison. Yet the very point of these truths is not to compare or judge them but simply (listening to Ereshkigal) to accept them. That truth – or the search for that truth – has been what brought us to the Underworld, and understanding that truth is what enables us to arise. This does not in any way alter the truth or maybe even the pain, but it will enable you to accept the bread and water of life.

For most of my own Descents I rarely was able to pinpoint the moment when the story swung about, at the time. Perhaps it is easier to do so as a witness of others' stories. Sometimes people have dramatic, near-death experiences; after which they are filled with great determination to survive and gratitude for life. Maybe someone says that one thing you needed to hear; or we find a book that does it for us; or a piece of music; or we pick up a paintbrush and begin creating; start a garden or write a poem. Sometimes we are shocked out of it; maybe by a death, an inner realization, pivotal dream or a declaration of love, anger or pain from someone we care for. Afterwards perhaps I can look back and say; *Oh, it was seeing the last sliver of the moon, that morning on the beach, before the sun rose, that was my turning point.* At the time I knew it was remarkable, but not that it was the single moment about which everything would revolve.

It seems unavoidable to note another great Descent and Ascent story here, that of Jesus. He is also involved with *the bread and water of life* (or bread and wine; and another of his stories involved the transformation of water into wine). I am entirely unqualified to discuss this, never having received any sort of religious instruction, or been a Christian. However, from my irreverent, Pagan and story-writer's perspective it looks like a match to me. Someone (God-like) dies, bread and water/wine are significantly invoked/involved and that someone rises from the dead.

Eat of this, it is my body; drink of this, it is my blood. In acts that represent the essence of life – drinking, eating – we consume what is dead and bring it to life again – the bread and water assume life by our consumption of them. They sustain our life and they are made alive by us. Christ arises through us, into us, through our consuming him. The bread and wine have animated him *because we have accepted them.* That is, if we left them sitting on the altar, unconsumed, he would not have arisen, he would not be within us. It is not enough that they exist, they must reach us and we must accept them, ingest them.

For ourselves, we will recognize turning points, even if only in retrospect. They are of absolute clarity, beyond doubt and beyond the stories we have been telling ourselves. They are moments that take us forward so completely there can after-wards be no going back. They are a veil ripped open, an express ride into the deep reality of our inner truth, a solution so neat and obvious it never occurred to us. Attendant with these moments is a lightness, a simplicity; some might call it the presence of angels. We take what moments earlier might have been considered an impossible step and we take it simply, quickly, lightly. Looking back seems irrelevant; we can no longer recognize the self we were before we took that step in understanding.

One of my own turning points revolved around my relationship with the Dark Goddess. For many years after that first conscious Descent of mine I felt trapped within the Underworld. Even when I struggled free – through the pure faith of putting one step in front of the next – I felt it always there at my back, ready to pull me under the second I hesitated. Using my – at that stage rudimentary – map, I was able to lead other women into their own places of darkness to meet the Dark Goddess there. I constructed rituals, workshops and articles around this knowledge of mine.

But each time I worked with her I paid a price. It didn't matter how many offerings I made – it didn't matter that I was essentially doing her work, the work of the Dark Goddess – every time I ran a Dark Goddess workshop I would get sick, my relationship would fall apart or I would encounter another loss in my life. I felt that the Dark Goddess was determined to devour me. I thought it was part of her nature, as indeed maybe it is. I pleaded with her.

During one Dark Goddess ritual, at the Chalice Well in Glastonbury (and I had done many Dark Goddess rituals there) I stepped right into her realm. The lid of the well was open and we were chanting as each woman gave an offering, or whispered into it, or sought to scry into its depths. There is a cast iron grid over the top of the well; the spaces in the grid are big enough to put your hand through. When it was my turn I knelt down before her, and then stood on top of the grid, above the well.

I felt her down there, in the swelling red waters; the depth of the faeries' otherworld; in the dark earth. I felt her power running all the way up through my body, ceaseless as the water that pounds through that spring and far far beyond what any mortal can hope to match and I put my foot down. Completely. It was as if the energy in that action continued beyond my foot, down into the well. And I felt her recede. Not vanish, but withdraw slightly. As I took on her energy I became her for an instant, and that instant was enough to change our relationship.

There was no disproportionate backlash from that ritual. Or from the following weekend, when I ran the Dark Goddess workshop. Or ever again. I don't think I could have done it earlier, years before. I didn't know how to do it. In that moment, that place, it happened. The world shifted, beneath my feet. I had assumed, for an instant, a power I did not have and for that instant I did have it. In that moment I became her; just as Inanna becomes her and Persephone becomes her and even mortal Psyche, opening the Goddess' box of beauty ointment becomes a Goddess. These are mysteries.

RITUAL: THE TURNING POINT

The intention of this ritual is to recognize your own turning point in the Underworld, where your Ascent begins.

This process is designed to take place AFTER the Listening to the Dark Goddess Ritual, *earlier in this section and when you have completed all you need to do in the Underworld on this particular journey.*

Time: 1 hour
You will need:
- Journal or paper and pen; coloring things optional
- Your altar
- Candle
- Optional – drum, rattle, chimes or other musical instrument

- Optional – incense, smudge
- The bread and water of life – (water and bread, or wine and crackers, or chocolate and pomegranate juice... for example)

Preparation

I think of this ritual as taking place on a dark moon, and by that I mean one of the three nights (preferably the middle one) that the moon is not visible in the sky. Some calendars call this a new moon – check and see if it is exactly half-way between the full moons to find out if they really mean dark moon. You don't have to do it on a dark moon, and you don't have to do it at midnight and you don't have to do it in a darkish room. But that's how I do it. To me, there's something special in having to wait (for the moon to be at that stage of its cycle, to wait up, feeling tired); maybe I connect it with Inanna waiting down there, for things to change. It makes it special, because I have gone to a particular effort and know it can't just be done anytime. Another advantage of working at this time is the quiet and lack of interruptions.

A different option is to find out the actual time of the dark moon, translate it into your local time (and there are websites that practically do this for you) and schedule your ritual for that time. Sometimes I have *felt* the moon shift into new. Of course your connection with the moon will be stronger – and thus make it more meaningful to do rituals at particular moon-times – if you look for the moon every day, come to know its rising and setting times and the places in the sky to look for it. In this way you can build up a whole relationship with the moon's cycle that is continuous – not one that just comes into play at full or new moon, but one that will teach you the different horizon points of rising and setting at different seasons and the angles the moon crosses the sky at these seasons, as well as the look of it at each stage.

The Ritual

Start your ritual about half an hour before you expect it to peak; whether that is at midnight or at the exact time of the dark moon, or any other time.

- Begin by tidying your altar and sitting before it, or if you prefer, you could do some stretches, vocal sounding or drumming.
- When you are ready, make your space sacred. You can do this by casting a circle, by smudging, toning or speaking a prayer or invocation to the Goddess. Then light the candle on your altar.
- Seated comfortably, breathe yourself into a light trance and begin to envisage the Underworld around you. Expand your awareness. You might feel the Underworld more than see it; sense it at the edges of your fingertips or become aware of a temperature change; or feel the air thickening. You might experience vivid images of underground caves and tunnels; or of the Dark Goddess.
- Allow your impressions and feelings to build, to swell around you. Allow them into your body. Breathe the air of the Underworld. Feel it on your skin. Feel the weight in your limbs, the numbness, the stillness. Imagine yourself into Inanna's story. There is Ninshubur, up above; send out a little thread to that part of yourself that retains conscious awareness, that will continue to look after your body even while you trance deeply. There is Ereshkigal, Queen of the Underworld, the only power this place recognizes. There are the *kurgarra* and the *galatur,* the tiny beings who have flown under the cracks in the Underworld gates to rescue Inanna. And there is Inanna's lifeless body, hanging on the meat hook.
- You are playing all the roles in this drama; the role of Ninshubur, loyally following directions; the role of Enki,

creating a method of escape; the role of the *kurgarra* and the *galatur*, unnoticeably slipping beneath your defenses and offering compassion; Ereshkigal with her moaning and groaning and Inanna, hanging in death until she is brought back to life. Try breathing into each of these characters one by one, to experience this scene from different perspectives. To do this, hold each one in your mind and as you breathe, imagine yourself slipping inside the skin of that character. Then try feeling what it is like, to be in that role in your Underworld drama. One of them may draw you much more strongly than the others, seeming to come to life as you breathe yourself into it. If this happens you can spend more time in that particular role.

- You might like to speak aloud while you are in these roles. Or make notes or drawings of how they feel. You might like to dance them, one by one; or sound them with your voice. Maybe you will draw them, or just feel deeply into them. But experience each one of them, remembering that compassion is the turning point of the myth. You must be able to witness your own suffering – or uncertainty, reluctance, fear or whatever it is – and feel compassion towards it. Towards yourself.

- Now begin to search for the turning point. Look around for it, feel through the myth for it, ask for it. Place your own life out there, in the Underworld; your own sense of not-knowing, of seeking. You might sense a spark to follow; you might become aware of the *kurgarra* and the *galatur*; you might feel the moon turn through the dark, or the earth towards the sun as midnight passes. You might have a sense of a new passage opening up in the Underworld; or of deadened limbs stirring again; of breath startling back into the body. When you get a sense of your turning point, make it louder/brighter/stronger in your imagination, or your inner eye. Imagine yourself getting ready to rise and take steps along this new path.

- Take up your ritual bread and water. You can sprinkle some crumbs from the bread and some drops of the water upon yourself if you like, although I prefer to eat and drink them. Allow the energy in the bread and water to enter into you.
- Remember at the end to ground the circle if you cast one and to put out any candles or incense you lit.

Sometimes, in ritual, one does not feel or experience the turning point. You can choose to continue following the form of the ritual – that is, to move onto the bread and water – and later (over the next few days) continue to ask and search for a turning point. An alternative response would be not to progress with the bread and water but to allow yourself to remain in the Underworld a little longer. You might repeat the ritual in a few days, in a week or even a month later if you have a strong feeling about staying longer in your Underworld state. Meanwhile you may spontaneously experience a turning point, which you could then choose to follow up with a ritual bread-and-water event, although that may not seem necessary to you.

In any case, however your ritual ends, make sure to spend some time recording it. If you are tired (if you have done it at midnight, for example) you might just jot a few notes down and record it more fully the next day. Recording a ritual like this is vital for later understandings. If I had not recorded my own attempts at a (backwards) Ascent, I might never have realized I actually did it backwards. Also, startling insights can arise that later retreat into semi-consciousness, denial or simple forgetfulness. Making a record allows you to reflect, and build on them later. By not clearly recording these kinds of events, we do ourselves – and later our friends and daughters – a disservice of not being able to show the way; at least the way we did it.

MAKING A MAP OF THE JOURNEY

The Underworld is under-mapped. Most of us are so pleased to be leaving that, like Inanna, we don't spare a backward glance. One of the great advantages of undertaking consciously chosen Underworld journeys is that we have a few more degrees of freedom, not being so insistently driven by a crisis. These degrees of freedom buy quite a lot in Underworld currency, including a clearer head, a stronger sense of direction and an increased ability to observe and record what we find down there.

This is a shadowy place, even at the best of times and making a map may seem to you inimical to the whole idea of being in the Underworld – handing oneself over to the mysteries; dissolving everything you knew and were – but the effort of map-making is worth it. Look at how eagerly we clutch at the stories of the myths, at any representation we find in art, music, theatre or fairytale of this baffling place that seems to exist both within us and outside us. Who dares draw a portrait of the Dark Goddess? Who will detail in words – poetry or journalism or short story – the worst moments of their lives as they confront their inner demons, meet their limitations and fall outside what is acceptable?

Anyone making a map of their own Underworld experience will do these things. At the very least it will confirm to them what they have experienced and understood. More, it will most probably assist them the next time they feel called – or dragged – to the Underworld. Shared in any form – spoken in a women's circle, shared with friends or relatives, used as a personal example in one's professional or creative life – it will serve as a genuine offering of self and a support for others. Published in any form – as theatre, in a blog, in an art exhibition, academic thesis or novel – it reaches out to the world, extending and deepening our collective knowledge of this denied and repressed segment of life. Any of these uses of your map is also an offering to the Dark Goddess herself; an offering that seeks to help rebalance our relationship with the dark; an offering that is a sacrifice in the deepest sense of making sacred.

Revisit the first two parts of your map; the map for Preparing to Descend and the map for Descending. Perhaps you have two long poems, and are ready to compose another. Or perhaps you have an embroidered altar cloth and a photo of a sand sculpture and have no idea how to express this third part of your map. Some suggestions follow, but remember it does not matter so much what form you chose, as the content you include. Your map should be able to show – at least to you – what it is like, in your Underworld, and the truths you met there.

Montage

Montages are wonderful, free-wheeling expressions of creativity. However planned they may have been (and some aren't planned at all) they have a way of growing themselves quite dynamically. The result is more than the sum of its parts and has a trick of capturing many shades and depths of meaning.

Montages are a work (usually flat but it could be 3D) made up of arranged, usually partially overlapping pictures. These are pasted onto stiff card or a board, although you could make one on your computer. Choose the size and shape of montage you want, before you begin. You will need pictures, drawings and photos; which you can collect from photo albums, magazines, postcards or images you've saved and you can draw some of them yourself. You'll also need scissors, glue for fixing the images onto the backing and some kind of finish over the top; a clear lacquer, a fixing spray or a sheet of glass if you are going to frame it. Optional extras include sparkle, ribbons, marking pens for decoration, highlighting and writing comments.

The ways a montage can be put together are limitless. You could start with your topic written in the centre of it, *The Underworld* and then spiral your images out towards the edges.

You could begin in one corner, cutting and pasting images and working on instinct; and just see what evolves. You could create a mandala in your montage, dividing it into sections and filling each one somewhat independently of the next. If you think your montage will be easily damaged, take a photo of it so you will retain this section of your map.

Underworld Evening Ritual

Create an evening ritual dedicated to the Underworld. For full effect you can do this on the dark moon. Maybe you will invite only one friend, or your whole women's circle; or you might choose to do it on your own. Spend part of the evening speaking of your own Underworld experience and record either it either on video or just with a voice recorder. You may invite others to speak of their Underworld experiences and if you have their permission, you can record those as well.

In your evening you can include such things as offerings to the Dark Goddess; silent meditation in the dark or with just a candle; and a ritual sharing of the bread and water of life. I always imagine the Dark Goddess is fond of dark chocolate, so I would include that as well. You might choose to dress in ritual robes, in black or in your finest regalia. Afterwards, find some way of keeping a record of your ritual, so that you retain this mapping of your Underworld experience.

Masks

I am both very resistant to, and love making masks. I'm resistant because I think I'm no good at it. I'm not artistic, it's difficult and fiddly and I'm certain I won't be able to make anything like what I imagine. I love it because, when I do it, such amazing creations have come forth.

I've made a black bird mask, using very stiff card and gold stitching; extremely simple, but utterly changing the shape of my head, as it comes forward to a beak well beyond my face. It has twigs of eucalyptus leaves sticking out the back like a cockatoo's crest. I've made a beast-of-the-fields mask, shaped a little like a horse's head, with impressionistic wheat fields painted on one side of it and jungle vines on the other. In place of the ears are owls' feathers on one side and long stalks of grass on the other. I've made a Dark Goddess mask out of a simple black eye-mask glued inside an elaborate, sequined decoration that was meant to be sewn into the neck of an evening dress, with its points sticking upwards, like a crown. I've made a liar's mask; one half black velvet, the other white lace, with tears of pearl beads dangling from ribbons on the dark side.

You can make an easy mask using stiff cardboard; a gourd cut open; a piece of tree bark; or fabric. You can also buy a basic or completely plain mask and decorate it however you will. Use paint and objects such as leaves, feathers, ribbons and old jewelry to embellish your mask. You can use elastic round the back, or make a mask that you hold up to your eyes, or put on a stick to hold in front of your face.

If you are making a mask for this part of your map you have a choice of subjects. You may choose to make a mask for Ereshkigal, or for Inanna/Ereshkigal; or for Persephone, or Psyche. You may choose to make one for the nameless, beyond-all-names Dark Goddess. You may choose to make a mask for yourself in the Underworld; or a set of matching masks; Inanna, Ninshubur and Ereshkigal, for example. The mask or masks should seek to express your time in the Underworld.

Once you've made the mask you can use it in ritual if you want. The *Gazing into the Mirror* ritual, in the next part of this book would be good to do in this mask. You can also place it on your altar, keep it among your ritual objects or put it on the wall. If you decide at some point to destroy your mask – or if it is quite fragile – take a photo of it so you retain a record of this part of your map.

PART FOUR:

COMING UP FROM THE UNDERWORLD

COMING UP FROM THE UNDERWORLD

Returning from the Underworld one travels back along the same route that one descended. Although in Egyptian mythology the path is circular, with the sun dying in the west each night and reborn to the east next morning, in both Greek and Sumerian mythology one retraces one's steps. Inanna goes back through each of the seven gates, collecting and resuming her powers and regalia at each gate. When she finally reaches the First Gate Ninshubur is waiting, just where Inanna left her. Psyche also carefully retraces her journey; back past the three-headed guard dog, back across the river on the ferry, back up the winding paths. Persephone's homeward journey is not so clearly detailed but she arrives back to the arms of her mother, which you could say was where she left from.

There is something deceptively easy about these mythical emergences from the Underworld, that I have not found to be true in my own life. Rather, I have felt returning to be like recovering from a severe illness. I imagine myself recovered only to find, one or three months later that no – *this* is what it feels like to be recovered – and to repeat that awakening several times, even over so long a period as a year or more. Oh, *now* I have returned fully from that Underworld place; oh *now* I am back... I begin to wonder if much of our time is not spent on the paths of the Underworld, either downwards or upwards and the much briefer periods are the pauses in between, fully down, or fully up. A little like breathing; where the in-breath and out-breath take up most of the time and the pauses between – with the breath fully in or fully out – are comparatively brief. With attention and practice one can learn to extend the pauses between breaths. Following on from this, I think we can learn to demarcate and even extend those times *above* and *below* – with attention and practice.

We can assist in the clarity of this process of demarcation by giving as much attention to the detail of returning, of ascending as we did to the descending. Thus even if we feel all our problems have been solved by the Descent itself, and our meeting with the Dark Goddess, still we should pay equal attention to arising and arriving back in the upper world. This final part of the journey contains the vital aspect of integration, where what we have understood and experienced becomes integrated into our lives. Sometimes this results in dramatic career, lifestyle or relationship changes or even an entire reorientation of the direction of our lives. Or it may manifest as layers of subtle reinterpretation and rebalancing. We all have a tendency to hurry over this part of the process, much as we have a tendency to linger over the Descent, delaying at all costs the furthering of each step. Neither of these tendencies – delaying Descents or hurrying Ascents – is conducive to understanding the true pattern of these journeys or assisting their transition.

In the stories of the Goddesses the motions of Ascent balance those of the Descent. This is most obvious in Inanna's case where she returns through the seven gates. Inanna appears to be in a hurry in both directions; her eagerness to descend is matched by her eagerness to get back; she's not the type for lingering journeys and would rather be where the action is. Persephone and Psyche are less obviously the mistresses of their own return. Psyche is in the process of shuttling obediently back to Aphrodite, until she suddenly defies her whole storyline by opening the mysterious box she is carrying. Both she and Inanna show there are still important things to be done on the way up.

What happens in real life when we take time out from the normal, upper world of social and economic activity? When we are ill; or when we take time off to go traveling (or write a book); or when we have a baby; in other words, when we step out from our ordinary routine for something profoundly personal, how are those experiences treated? Rarely are we willing or able to put the time in to properly or fully prepare. Mostly we try to squeeze that preparation in amongst our usual activities. Even whilst becoming seriously ill – how soon do we stop what we are doing and begin to pay it all the attention it requires? As soon as possible? Or – as late as possible? When we are utterly forced to? And how soon do we expect to recover? More or less instantly? The same is often true for having a baby; commonly women work up until the last minute. Or we expect the pregnancy just to somehow fit in with everything else we are doing; including looking after older children. Once we've had the baby – bang! – all should return to normal. Even with travel I have noticed how hardly anyone is interested in what I saw or experienced 'over there'. They just want me to slot back into my ordinary life, quickly.

The world we have created does not encourage or promote leave-of-absences. It does not promote deep contemplation, especially the type with no time-frame. If absence must be granted – for illness, birth, travel – just exactly the time it takes will be extended, with very little preparation time and the minimum of recovery time. This is obvious when we look at our attitude to depression (quite a common occurrence) – fight it off however you can, and if you succumb, get back as quick as possible – to inner contemplation (surely necessary in most people's lives) – fit it into a weekly yoga lesson, a daily meditation practice, a week's holiday retreat – and as for Descents - ! These more sacred, devotional, merely personal or interior aspects of life are expected to be fitted into and around the main business of life, not to dictate to it. As much as ascending slowly and carefully is straining society's tolerance for our absence (including the tolerance of our partner, friends and family), part of the whole process is creating and extending our *own* tolerance for being temporarily out of the loop.

Whereas the Descent may not have felt like our choice, over an Ascent we can take much more conscious control. Our arrival will bring spring, we can afford to step carefully. We can acknowledge each piece of our lives as we regain access to it and find a new way of wearing, carrying or relating to it. We can pause between gates. We can choose which boxes to open; even those we have been told by our elders never to open at any cost. This care is also a way of nurturing whatever it is you are bringing up from the Underworld; be it your rediscovered yearning to be a healer; recognition of your unique self; or the need for change. Rather than thrust what you have retrieved (or who you have become) out into the world, you get time for gradual acclimatization and adjustment.

Coming up can be trickier than going down. Going down is like falling, once you've begun, there's a certain amount of gravitational inevitability about it, and an obvious direction. You can delay if you like, but there's no disputing that down is down. Whereas up is trickier. Any degree of up-ness, having being on the bottom, can seem so blessed and light-filled that one doesn't see one hasn't fully emerged yet. It takes its own time. If there's a fast path here, a short cut, I haven't learned it. And perhaps it's important to take it slowly, to integrate each step of the return, piece by piece. I've never been particularly fast at anything, so probably it's just my nature to return so slowly, but unlike delays on the way down, I don't think these delays are a disability.

I write that, but immediately I can see how they could be. If one was coming off an addictive drug for instance, emerging from that particular place of darkness, one would not wish to be delayed endlessly on the levels of emergence. One would have to take some firm hand in the program. Or if one was rehabilitating from a disease or accident, it wouldn't be so great to just sit around waiting for things to improve. An accident victim has to undergo rehabilitation, physiotherapy, enforced exercise – whatever it takes, what is presented as the methodology of emerging – an addict has to stick to a program of releasing herself from the drugs – without necessarily (yet) feeling good about it.

At a certain point in the story – when one is no longer actually dead – one has to start taking steps. Keep going, upwards through gate after gate after gate until finally one is emerged. Then there's all those demons whirling about your skirts; but keep going. Greet your loved ones, tell them what they mean to you and keep going. Meet the hard places where things have come unstuck, bring your insights and courage and knowledge to them, and keep going. Mourn your losses, grieve, make amends where appropriate; keep going. The story does not stop and you are the central force of your Ascent. When you stop, you may as well be back with Ereshkigal, in the Underworld, on the meat hook.

Contrariness in the Underworld

The myths mirror the urgency, the obscurity, the necessity and the mystery of what goes on for us in our personal Underworld journeys. We're looking for something that can't be found in our ordinary lives, in the upper world. Sometimes, like Psyche, we've been sent down there; by a Goddess, a wise counselor, creative inspiration, a crisis or a bleak, bloody reality we can't escape. Echoing Persephone's story we might imagine we've been abducted, or we may suspect we are searching for hidden truths. Like Inanna, we might be so sure of our own powers that we march in there, demanding recognition and special treatment.

We know we're looking for something – a key, the way out, understanding, transformation – though we can't exactly say what form it will come in or what the end result will look like. There's generally a lot of weeping, moaning and groaning as we struggle to give birth to something; a new part of ourselves or a new path in our life. We can't leave until we have done this – and everything down there is very slow, very dark and can be very difficult. Even the simplest things become, sometimes, nearly impossible.

We have to step outside what we've been told. We have to break the rules. Propriety. What is accepted, or acceptable. We have to do things we wouldn't normally do; take risks. These risks do not involve hurting or endangering anyone else. They only place you, the risk-taker outside the known. Psyche opens the box of beauty ointment that only a Goddess can tolerate. The story's action speeds up and almost immediately she is made a Goddess. Inanna ventures into the Underworld, from which no-one returns. Three days later, she returns. Persephone eats the food of the Underworld, which ensures she can never leave. Almost immediately, she leaves the Underworld.

We might have to act as if we already had the powers we need. If Psyche hadn't opened the box of beauty ointment she wouldn't have died on those Underworld paths. Perhaps she never would have been reunited with her lover, or made her way to the court of the Gods, where Zeus grants her immortality. If Persephone hadn't eaten the pomegranate seeds maybe she would have been returned – a maiden, still nameless and not a queen – to her mother's loving (endless) embrace. Or maybe she would have been stuck, a shade amongst other shades in the Underworld, between one state and another.

Inanna disobeyed all the local wisdom to set out for the Underworld. But perhaps if she hadn't been hanging on a meat hook in the Underworld, Ereshkigal wouldn't have been in labor. If Ereshkigal hadn't been in labor perhaps Inanna couldn't have been born again, at any price. There's a contrariness in the actions of these mythic characters. Against all advice, logic and sense they take an irredeemable step – and it turns out that exact step is the transition to the next level of the myth, to the integration of their powers and the conclusion. It may turn out that the thing you have been denying yourself, the illogical, unsenscial thing is the exact thing that will propel you forward in your own story, into – and through – the Underworld.

Transactions occur in the Underworld. Things change hands,

change form, change places. The myth is at some crucial, dire, sticking point – Psyche opening the box, Persephone eating the seeds, Inanna dead on a meat hook – and then, instead of the expected result a twist occurs. That is – the expected does happen – Psyche dies, Persephone is condemned to remain forever in the Underworld, Inanna has been murdered – and then the *unexpected* turns out to be wedded to that very same event. In a twist of paradox it is that very action that *caused* oblivion that causes renewal. It is death that brings life. Winter that brings spring. The out-breath that brings the in-breath.

In myth this transition does not happen casually. Only once everything is lost does rescue occur. Only once there is no longer any way out does a way out appear. Only when the known is utterly exhausted is the unknown born from it. Without this transition from one set of realities to a new set of realities Ereshkigal would still be laboring and Inanna dead. Persephone's world would still be in winter, or – conversely, if Demeter had had her way – an endless summer. Psyche would still be weeping and wailing, performing impossible tasks for a demanding Aphrodite. Inanna would be Queen of Heaven and Earth, and Ereshkigal Queen of the Underworld but the sisters would be split, still; with no integration of life and death.

These transformations are remarkable. In each case, the Goddess (at least) doubles her realms of power. Psyche becomes a Goddess, though before she was a mortal woman. Inanna becomes the only being to have – under her own steam, so to speak – willingly entered and successfully arisen from the Underworld. Not long after she has sent her consort to replace her in the Underworld, she is able to decree a very unorthodox arrangement – that Dumuzi's sister will replace *him* in the Underworld for six months of every year. Inanna now has the power to cause not only life, but death, and even periodic death. Persephone doesn't, strictly speaking, die in her Underworld. But she loses her maidenhood, a sort of ritual death. She has ceased to be primarily a daughter and become Queen of the Underworld.

In each case there was an initiator. In Inanna's case Ereshkigal reacts with glee upon learning Inanna is foolish enough to seek entry into the Underworld. She ruthlessly enacts the initiation of her sister, up to and including her death. Aphrodite has set Psyche task after impossible task. Hecate stood back, aware of Persephone disappearing into the Underworld but saying nothing about it for quite a long time. These Goddesses – older and/or darker and certainly more powerful within the realms we are discussing are playing a crucial role. They are the initiators. They could have prevented all the difficulties; stayed their hands, intervened, made things easier. Not only would there not be any story had they done this, there also would have been no process. Psyche would still be a silly girl in love with a God. Persephone might still be trailing around after her mother, wondering why she had no name or role of her own. Inanna would be forever estranged from her sister and half of the powers of the Great Goddess.

Those experiences – those Descents, deaths/consummations – are what it took. The initiator acts not from cruelty but from necessity. The necessity of creating, or allowing what it takes for the integration that comes with Descent. A Descent is a fallow period followed by rapid growth. Look at the descent of a seed. It falls off the tree – or goes through whatever process it goes through (sometimes being partially digested, for instance) – to end up in the earth, the Underworld. Only down there can it reach its potential. After a period of stasis it comes to life and struggles back into the upper world. Its roots remain down there, in the dark, to nourish and sustain it, and literally as foundations to hold it up. Before, it was nothing, almost nothing; potential, that's all. One in millions. But now it is fully alive and forever wedded to the Underworld, as well as the upper world.

Integration

When Inanna, Persephone and Psyche emerge from the Underworld things have crucially changed, and not only within themselves. There's been a rebalancing of power, an almost unimagined integration down there in the Underworld and upon re-emergence, everything shifts around to accommodate that. The Goddess is like the shuttle in a piece of weaving. When she is below, changes happen below, finalizing in some kind of ingestion; and as she ascends integration begin to happen above, to bring about a necessary balance with the Underworld and reflect the changes she has undergone.

For Persephone the whole terrain has changed, literally. She left a summerland to return to a much more conditional place, encompassing the regular hardships, privations and dying off that winter brings. Psyche's return plays out on a more personal level. Down on the paths of the Underworld she assumed the stature of a Goddess, when she opened the box of beauty ointment meant only for a Goddess. Now she has become a Goddess; far removed from her former home, family and uncertain status as the mortal lover of a God. Inanna returns from her Underworld sojourn to find a palace revolution; her beloved consort Dumuzi has taken advantage of her absence to set himself up on her throne. She performs an action mirroring Ereshkigal's greeting of herself, earlier on; consenting as the train of demons who've dogged her since she left the Underworld seize hold of her disloyal lover. They drag him off to become her replacement and begin the next episode of this cyclic drama.

In each one of these stories the changes wrought in the Goddess while she was in the Underworld cause ripple effects in the world. Even in our own stories we can expect this to happen. We have been through an intense experience in our own Underworld, even if it has seemed to be very drawn-out, perhaps with much time spent hanging on a meat hook, traversing labyrinthine paths or merely waiting for release to be granted.

Nonetheless this is not a simple return of having been lost and now restored. Immense and often fundamental change has occurred. Perhaps it looks like only one little thing has happened – you ate a few pomegranate seeds, that's all – and yet the repercussions are not simple at all. Something integral has altered within you and thus nothing can remain the same on your return.

Change that occurred in the Underworld is mirrored by changes brought back to the upper world. There's a saying, *As above, so below*. Perhaps it should really be, *As below, so above*. It is in the Underworld these changes have been birthed, and it is direct from the Underworld these agents – Persephone, Inanna, Psyche – come to instigate change in the upper world. A Descent can be a quiet thing, unnoticed by many as the descending woman slips below the surface of her life, caught in a rip-tide of necessity, or diving deep to explore the depths. I do not think an Ascent can be so quiet.

Having lost – or given away – everything, on the way down; changes may not appear so frightening to us as they might otherwise have been. We have been changed – or revealed – in the very essence of ourselves and it seems inevitable circumstances must change to accommodate this. However it often does not appear so inevitable to those around us. Like Demeter, they may have been expecting us to return unchanged; or like Dumuzi they may even have taken advantage of our absence. Like Aphrodite or Eros they may have assumed we were lost. These attitudes do not result in readiness for the consequences of our return. We have been through the teeth of change in that Descent, gate by gate relinquishing everything dear to us. We have been held helpless, digested by the forces of the Underworld and we have been pierced through to the core by the eyes of the Dark Goddess; eyes whose vision and understanding we now share. To come back from such a journey and begin to make changes in our lives is inevitable, but to all around us it may seem an unwelcome disaster.

This is another instance of what we battled originally, hearing that call; the resistance of the dark. Perhaps not issuing from ourselves this time, but from those we tore ourselves away from, in order to be able to make the journey in the first place. When we come back and begin to rewrite ourselves or our lives, all around us may scream at the injustice of it. Inanna's sons were saved from having to replace her in the Underworld, but her consort Dumuzi was not. Later his sister, also, has to undergo the same journey. In Persephone's story she herself is bound to repeated journeys into what is now her own realm of the Underworld. Psyche is uplifted, deified, but her daughter is born mortal and therefore, like all mortals, doomed to death and the Underworld.

Not everyone is happy with the results of this integration. Dumuzi is distraught – and more or less destroyed, until later his sister rescues him – and Inanna herself goes into a period of deep mourning over her lost lover, even though it was she who cast him to his fate. Demeter obviously never (to this day) gets over the periodic loss of her daughter to the Underworld, allowing a further winter to occur each time Persephone returns to her own realm; a coherent reminder to the rest of the Gods on Olympus – not to mention us mortals – of her potency and the power of her displeasure. As for Psyche; it is not mentioned what Aphrodite's response to the outcome is, but Psyche and Eros have to balance their own immortality with their daughter's mortality; surely no easy task.

It's as if the very act of integration of our own Underworld experience tips, domino-like, against others we are close to, possibly requiring them to undertake their own journeys and integration. This could be endless and indeed our simplest model, that of the moon which dies away into darkness and is then reborn; is not a single instance, but cyclic and continual. Past the full there is another dying and rebirth, and another and another. A single Descent is part of a natural process; the entire natural process is continual Descents and Ascents.

Just before I began working on the final section of this book I had a dream where it was explained to me, quite patiently, that the story of Inanna and Ereshkigal was the perfect story for the earth at this time. Inanna represented the Earth itself; all the bright beauty of the living, growing, magnificent diversity of plants, animals, insects; she was the clear skies with the shining sun, the stars that seem so magical to us; she was all of our human living, loving, struggling and creating. Queen of Heaven and Earth – but she was not exactly Queen, more she was *it*, heaven and earth; she was life itself. I felt it briefly, like the Charge of the Star Goddess (and Inanna, who in her own time was Venus, the morning and evening star is surely a Star Goddess); *I who am the beauty of the green earth, and the white moon amongst the stars and the mystery of the waters...* For a moment, I was all that, in its fullness, beauty and life.

Then I was shown Ereshkigal. Ereshkigal is what we are facing. Global warming; increasingly extreme and frequent natural disasters; extinction of many species (perhaps most, or even all); a rising spiral of likelihood that control of anything (everything) will be wrested out of human hands and beyond our choices (way beyond). She was the black hole of oblivion we were speeding towards. And yet – who knows? Perhaps on the very brink something new will reveal itself, some way to steer around the outside circuits of complete destruction. Perhaps – otherwise – we will enter the black hole, the one-way street past the point of no return, and then – after she has hung us on the meat hook of our own arrogance – what then? Will she give birth to us again? Will we meet our soul, in that dark place?

INANNA'S ASCENT

When the *kurgarra* and the *galatur* sprinkle the food and water of life upon Inanna, she arises. Her body – that has been dead, an empty shell – animates and Inanna is alive again. She departs the realm of the Underworld immediately and progresses back up through the seven gates. Her robe is returned to her at the Seventh Gate; her lapis measuring rod and line at the Sixth Gate; her armband at the Fifth Gate; her breastplate at the Fourth Gate; her double strand of beads at the Third Gate; her necklet at the Second Gate and her crown at the First Gate so that when she emerges she is fully arrayed again in the adornments of her power. Once again she is Inanna, Queen of Heaven and Earth.

Something else comes with her, though, from the Underworld. A train of demons, clinging to her skirts. These demons will not allow Inanna to resume her life just as it was before she descended to the Underworld. They have come with her for a specific purpose; to find her replacement. For no-one can descend to the Underworld and return, that is the rule, and in the bending of this rule for Inanna, someone must be found to take her place. Ninshubur, still waiting by the First Gate is the first one the demons seize, though Inanna holds them off and denies them her loyal retainer. As they all progress back across the land to Inanna's cities (the places where her temples are) the demons seize first her eldest son and later her younger son. Both sons have been in mourning for Inanna and both of them she protests she cannot lose to the Underworld. The demons don't mind, they know they will get someone in the end.

These demons are still with her when Inanna reaches her own city and discovers Dumuzi, her consort and beloved, sitting on her throne. He is not in mourning and seems to be having a fine time in her absence. When the demons seize him, Inanna speaks no words of protest. Instead, in a neat integration of Ereshkigal's powers, she turns on him that Eye of Death she herself met in the Underworld and allows him to be taken. She has assumed an aspect of Ereshkigal, has carried Ereshkigal up with her. Hers was the Eye of Death, for him; hers the word of death. Just as Ereshkigal gave symbolic birth to Inanna down in the

Underworld, in the upper world, Inanna incarnates an aspect of her dark sister and – further – sends her own lover down to Ereshkigal. Back at the beginning of the story Inanna said she was visiting the Underworld to follow the mourning rites of her sister's husband; and so, since she was culpable in Gugulana's death, it is like the final piece in the jigsaw when she sends her own husband to her sister, and to death.

Imagining Inanna
I return from the Underworld triumphant.

Dead I have been and am alive. Decayed was my body, that now is beautiful again. Helpless was I, that now am filled with power.

I have been through the seven circles of hell. Cold they were, and each one colder. As I descended through each gateway I lost more and more of myself, until I was a wraith, a shadow, a slender memory. I was lucky to escape spending eternity there.

I am Inanna and I have died to rise again as Queen and Goddess. I am Inanna and I return, triumphant to my city.

My companion Ninshubur is with me, loyal as my heart My two sons are with me, loyal as my left hand and my right hand. Around us cluster the demons of the Underworld. They are seeking a life to replace mine. I will not give them my beloved Ninshubur, who brought me out of the Underworld. I will not give them my first son for he mourned my death and rejoices at my life. I will not give them my second son, for he also mourned my death and rejoices at my life.

I enter my city and all who see us bow down in mortal terror. I have returned from death, and yet. How have I lived, but by promising the death of another? And the demons flow about me, entreating me to choose. Who will die that Inanna may live? I enter my precinct and the very trees seem to lean away from our path. I enter my gardens and hear laughter. Why is the palace not in mourning? Inanna departed for the Underworld three days past and has not been heard of. If Inanna is gone, how dare any rejoice?

I advance with my deadly retinue. We stand and observe the inner gardens. There is a feast, musicians, guests. My throne is there, the throne of Inanna. My husband Dumuzi sits upon it, he is raising a cup of wine to his lips. Women lie around him, in the grass by the trees. They are eating and singing, they are half naked. No-one is in mourning.

The demons flood about me in a black cloud and seize Dumuzi. I open my mouth. I look at my husband. I prepare to say: Not him! You cannot have Dumuzi! *and instead my voice cries out:* Yes! Take him! Take Dumuzi! *and the demons whirl about and pull him off the throne.*

Dumuzi, tumbled on the ground, is frightened. He cries out to me.

Save me, Inanna! *he cries.* Do not let them take me!

The demons turn to me. I look around. Slowly I look. I see the food laid out, the cups of wine, my throne and the women huddled together by the trees. I see Dumuzi trembling with fear on the ground.

Take him! *I cry.* Take Dumuzi away!

And he was taken.

MY OWN INANNA STORY: ASCENDING

Our Ascent process began pre-dawn on the third day, following the pattern of the dark moon and of Inanna, who spends three days in the Underworld. (Easter also follows that pattern remembering, or sometimes re-enacting, Christ's death each year.) The plan was to go up through the seven gates, receiving back our regalia at each gate. Someone came to wake me at about 4:30am. I rose and went to the side door of the Temple, the place where only a few nights before I had wept by the fire. I knew something had turned, something had changed but I did not know entirely what. I undressed in the cold darkness and went into the hall.

Ereshkigal was not there. I felt her absence in the dim light, or maybe it was her presence, within me now. Naked I went to the Seventh Gate and my robe was handed to me, by hands I could barely see. I put it on, the fabric rough on my skin. At the Sixth Gate my measuring rod and line was returned to me and as I grasped it, I felt certainty settling within me. Still a writer. Fifth

Gate; the snake armband – a small flare of delight in my sexuality – and then Fourth Gate; the breast-plate. Settling it around me, tying its ribbons at the side I had a moment to recognize the paradox I had made; vulnerability and strength. My strength is in vulnerability. Third Gate; and I receive back my double strand of beads, compassion. Second Gate; my small string of beads is handed to me, my connections in the world.

I come to the final, First Gate. It is the double wooden doors that lead outside. My crown is handed to me and I place it on my head. The doors swing open and I step forwards. The doors face East and a glimmer of sun is on the horizon. Rays of light shoot through the trees towards me. There are women, around, beside me and my High Priestess, who led us all fearlessly through this extraordinary process. She gives me a five-fold blessing and speaks words that are utterly strange to me, nothing I ever expected to hear in my lifetime.

She is anointing me as a Priestess of the Goddess. The words drip into my ears with singular, amazing clarity, everything is very slow and I know I have a moment, a second to choose, to say *yes* or *no*. I look down these future paths from where I stand, at their division. Both of them are lit by the rays of the rising sun. One of them is the path I have expected to take. It looks familiar. Still exciting – I am young and most things are yet to discover. The other path, which I see as branching off to the left, I never dreamed of. Before this moment I did not know it existed. I have no idea what it is composed of. Before the last few days I might not even have recognized it. It is the path where I am a Priestess of the Goddess.

Yes, I breathe and step onto the unknown path. There was complete clarity – complete choice – and I had no hesitation. The rising sun called to me and I stepped forward. Wonder, yes; but no doubt. For me it is momentous; one of the truly pivotal moments of my life but for others watching it is expected, ordinary. After receiving a blessing as a Priestess of

Inanna/Ereshkigal – and I wonder how many of them have been ordained in the last two thousand years – I stand to one side and watch the remaining four or five women come through the final gate, and receive the blessing in their turn. I look at them closely and though they are all moved, I cannot pick up any lives changing direction in those seconds, like mine did. But perhaps I would not see it, for someone else. The sun has risen by now; I was the one who met that particular small miracle, this day.

That was the map, the first time I undertook the journey. Not that I had not descended before – I often thought half my life, at least, had been lived in the Underworld. The world of dreams, of imagination, of the inner workings; a world where one's own truth is unrecognizable in the outside world. But I had never had a map before, or any idea that there was a map. I had never understood the Underworld was a place one could visit deliberately, and return from with some sort of grace.

From that point, slowly and inevitably, my life changed; swung round like a compass point seeking a direction. I continued to be a writer; I am still a writer. But a second, great part of my life opened up; the part I had never imagined. I became a Priestess of the Goddess; firstly in name, secondly within myself and finally in the outside world. The integration of this took many years, and even now I am still learning to walk fully within it. There were many years simply of discovery; of learning my magic, of discovering ritual, of forming and joining women's groups, of reading more and more of myth, magic and the Goddess and this time not reading it from academic interest but real and lived knowledge. There followed many more years; creating and offering rituals and women's groups; developing workshops; writing articles; beginning to run regular groups.

Eventually there is this; joining my first vocation of writer up with my second, of Priestess. This is what Ereshkigal birthed in me on that great, ritualistic Descent, and this is the form it has taken. She found an expression for a part of me that had never had a clear channel, an outlet. I had always identified with women, always spoken to trees and rivers, always loved and felt the life of mythology, always yearned for real magic; but never – before my Descent – did I have a way to make those things real in my life; real and lived and living. That concept, that job description, that initiation of *priestess* gave me that.

RITUAL: GAZING INTO THE MIRROR
The intention of this ritual is to meet the Dark Goddess.

Time: 1 hour

You will need:

- A hand mirror, or if unavailable, a wall mirror
- Journal, or paper and pen
- Drawing things

Preparation

By now you have many understandings about the role of the Dark Goddess. Consider the parts of your life that fall under her auspices. Maybe you think of her as a source of power, inspiration or of change. Many women feel they have a special dedication, or belonging to the Dark Goddess. You may feel you were born with this; or that you chose it; that you have always known it or you are just now coming to understand it. You may feel that the Dark Goddess has overwhelmed your life, or directed you along particular paths you no longer wish to take.

Although the Dark Goddess can be understood as any (or all) of the actual, named Goddesses who are associated with the Underworlds of different cultures, she can also be understood as a force of nature and of life. We usually experience her as external to ourselves. Many of our experiences of Descent resemble being dragged, protestingly, away from our normal life by events and circumstances beyond our control. Confronting the Dark Goddess feels very like facing the frightening witch all the fairy stories warn against; like the demons and monsters of our imagination.

The Dark Goddess is not at all like us; in short, she is scarily *other*. We have a lot riding on the differentiations. She is scary and we are not; she is angry, or hidden or implacable or in agony and we are not. She is powerful and we... Somewhere the separation starts to fall apart, as we begin to admit well, sometimes we are like that. Even, we might want to be like that, or at least borrow some of her qualities. We might even concede that our view of her could be distorted. But still we are viewing her as external to ourselves. If we cannot find the Dark Goddess in our own eyes, looking out of the mirror at us, we will not be able to see her truth anywhere else. Recognizing her within yourself is a further step towards bringing a balance between the light and the dark, and towards integrating your Underworld experience. It is this knowledge that she is within us, as well as outside us that enables us to integrate her gifts and her energy, and so complete our return from the Underworld.

The Ritual

- Choose a way to create sacred space for your ritual; by casting a circle, lighting a candle on your altar, speaking aloud a prayer or invocation to the Dark Goddess or some other method.

- Write down a list of the areas of your own life that fall within the realms of the Dark Goddess. You might include such things as sleep, night, dreams, healing, mystery, the unknown, initiation, birth, death, renewal. There may also be more personal areas that you consider fall within the realm of the Dark Goddess; your creativity, your empathy or your psychic abilities. If you are not entirely sure of some, you can mark those items with a question mark, or have a different list for them.

- In a sentence or two sum up your relationship to the Dark

Goddess. You might want to use words such as *initiate, acolyte* or *priestess*; or you might describe your relationship with her as *unknown; frightening; compelling* or *repugnant.* Add a sentence on what you would like your relationship to become; maybe one of greater understanding, respect or recognition.

- If you have a strong association with one or more of the named Dark Goddesses – such as Ereshkigal, Persephone, Hecate, Morgan le Fay, the Black Madonna – write her name, or their names down. For each name you've written, list a few main points that you associate with this aspect of the Dark Goddess.

- Choose one of your named Dark Goddesses, or if you did not have any, work with the Dark Goddess herself, and make a drawing of her energy. It need not be a figurative drawing – it can be purely color and shape. Find a way of expressing your awareness of her that is not in words. After you've finished the drawing, look at it again. Does it show you anything more about the Dark Goddess, or your relationship to her? If you learn something new, make a note of it.

- Spend a few moments settling and becoming aware of your breathing. Slow your individual breaths down and become aware of their rhythms. Think of regularizing your breathing, so that each in-breath and out-breath are of similar length, with pauses between each one. You can count to assist yourself; six beats for an in-breath; two before you start to breathe out; six beats for the out-breath and a further two before you begin to breathe in again. You can visualize the breath entering and leaving your body; some people imagine it as a particular color or density. If you are tense or distracted now is the time you will notice it most, as you may have to struggle to keep your attention on your breath. If your mind wanders, or your breath speeds up or becomes irregular, bring your attention gently back to it.

- When your breathing is calm and regular pick up your hand mirror (or move to the wall mirror). Gaze into the mirror, allowing your focus to soften and even blur. If you find yourself examining your face (checking your make up or finding little imperfections) close your eyes for a moment and return to your breathing pattern. Seek to still your mind, and reach within yourself for a feeling of quiet. Then try the gaze again.

- Once you have a soft-focus gaze, begin to look into your own eyes. Imagine you are seeing into the depths of them. Notice all the little details; flecks of color, the changing width of your pupils, the absolute particularities of your eyes. You can choose one eye to focus on, if you find that easier.

- Begin to seek the Dark Goddess within the depths of your eyes. Dive into the darkness there, sense it expand and begin to reveal hints of its secrets. *Ask* to see her. Sometimes you will catch a flash of something that feels greater than yourself; some people have a vision of something completely beyond themselves and others may just have a sense of something stirring – or hidden – or see nothing at all. Persist, even if you see nothing.

- If you do see, or sense the Dark Goddess in your eyes, you may choose to ask her a question, or tell her something. Even if you do not see or sense her, you may still do this, and see your own eyes reflecting back to you. You may choose just to sit in silence and regard her, or regard what part of herself she has revealed. If you do not see anything special, it may be that the very blackness and hiddenness is showing you something of your relationship towards the Dark Goddess. Spend about ten minutes gazing into the mirror.

- To conclude the ritual, write some notes about what happened for you; or if you prefer, make another drawing.
- Ground and complete your ritual by undoing any steps you took to create a sacred space. Ground your circle, speak a prayer of thanksgiving to the Dark Goddess, blow out the candle on your altar or do whatever else is appropriate to conclude your ritual.

This ritual can be repeated if you like; either as part of a longer ritual or just to take you further into that experience of finding and meeting the Dark Goddess within yourself. Connecting with her in this deep way is a significant step on from viewing her as something external to ourselves, beyond our reach or unknowable. This is a beautiful ritual to do with a group of women; sharing your experiences after gazing into the mirror. You can each have your own mirror, or take turns in passing the mirror around the circle or standing before it.

ASCENTS IN OTHER MYTHS
Psyche
Psyche is close to achieving the fourth of the four impossible tasks the jealous Aphrodite has set her. But then, still in the labyrinthine paths of the Underworld, she opens the mysterious box she is carrying; a beauty ointment sent from one Goddess to another. It was not meant for mortal women and what was she thinking? She falls down dead.

Maybe she was thinking along similar lines to Persephone, when she ate those pomegranate seeds? Or Inanna, when she ventured down to the place no-one ever returned from?

Defying all logic these are the moments that make the story, and in Psyche's case prompt her long lost lover into action. Eros swoops down into the Underworld paths and back into the story. He picks up Psyche's body, flying her straight to Mount Olympus and a court of the Gods. One has to wonder why he did not take such action earlier; or why all of his actions until now have involved hiding (hiding Psyche away, hiding his true identity, hiding himself from Psyche when she transgresses his requirements). What learning has he been through, while Psyche labored at her tasks? Or was this simply her initiation, which he could not interfere with, until the last?

Zeus, the sole arbiter, declares the lovers may be together and returns Psyche to life, now immortal life. What might seem a humiliation for the Goddess of Love, Aphrodite, having to give up her son in marriage to a girl she has long done her best to keep him from, is a victory for Love. The role Aphrodite has played is not unlike Ereshkigal's role for Inanna; that of initiator. In the versions of the myth we have been handed down this clearly was not her intention. But actions speak louder than words and Aphrodite's actions have carried Psyche to this place. On that basis I believe it was – if not exactly her intent – at least her purpose. She has played out the role of the Goddess of Love, to initiate her acolyte into divine love.

There is just one catch. Psyche is pregnant at the time of this deliberation and although Zeus promises immortality to the child if it is a boy, if it is a girl he declares she will remain mortal. We could see this as an early case of sex discrimination but there's also a certain inevitability here. The child is a girl who is named Joy. So Eros (love) and Psyche (soul) are immortal, but the joy born to them is mortal and dies. Each generation, each being must undertake the journey for themselves. The mysterious beauty ointment sought from Persephone as Queen of the Underworld – possibly mortality itself – which was Psyche's lot earlier, is passed on to her daughter. Thus the story is completed and begun again.

Persephone
Persephone's story also is both completed and begun again when she emerges from the Underworld. Her arrival is the event that

ends winter upon the earth. Demeter's quest for her daughter's return is fulfilled and she can resume her duties as mistress of grain and field. Yet Persephone's cyclic Descent in a few months time will bring with it the onset of another winter. Persephone – and Demeter's response to Persephone's absences – has set in train the Wheel of the Year – when she departs autumn will arrive; when she returns, there will be spring. The drama of Persephone is played out on a planetary level.

Persephone has also integrated other things down there in the dark. Pomegranate seeds that she ate whilst in the Underworld – famous for being the ostensible reason she could not return forever to be with her mother – seem to point to her own pregnancy, to the Lord of the Underworld and yet another integration – from being simply the daughter she is moving into the realm of being a mother herself. This reveals older aspects of the myth, where Demeter and Persephone are seen as two aspects of one Goddess.

Initiation by the Dark Goddess

Studying the fairytale of Snow White I became aware of the motif of a young woman being initiated by an older, more powerful, Queen or Dark Goddess figure. The Queen, Snow White's step-mother, provides an initiation – admittedly a very severe one, but traditional in its symbolism – a death and rebirth experience. Snow White undergoes three near-death experiences, or four if you include her encounter with the hunter, which can be seen as the call to initiation. All of these experiences are provided by the Queen and in this light the Queen can also be seen as the Dark Goddess, whose challenge cannot be avoided.

Snow White's transition is from a helpless child at the mercy of others to an adult woman with the friendship and loyalty of the dwarves; her own court. The ending of her story is a fairytale marriage with a prince. A Jungian reading would say this is the development of Snow White's animus and the integration of her self. Or an initiatory reading would point to her transition into Queendom, a state parallel with her persecutor (or initiator), the original Queen, her step-mother.

This understanding completely changed the story for me and began to remind me of other tales where a powerful feminine character – portrayed as negative, or even evil – actually provides the catalyst for the younger female character to find freedom, love and power through rising to the challenges presented to her. In short, an initiation into womanhood. This takes the form of meeting the more powerful feminine force on its own terms; changing or rewriting the terms she has dictated and, vitally, integrating some of her power – power that was initially used against the young woman – into her own character and actions.

In Snow White's story the Queen's apparent attempts to murder her actually result in Snow White's removal from the Queen's immediate sphere of power, thus providing Snow White a space to find her own power. Later the Queen even looses her status in interactions with Snow White; reduced to presenting herself as a crone or beggar or a kind of door-to-door sales-woman. The Queen's power is apparently wrapped up in her beauty, and as Snow White's beauty rivals that of the Queen, it is underwritten that therefore so does her power. This beauty – or power – then allows Snow White to win the love of the prince and thus become completely safe from the Queen; an ending which can be interpreted in various ways. But in all of those ways one thing is clear. Snow White has survived, has taken on the challenges set her and has been initiated by the Dark Goddess.

In another fairytale a Queen turns six – or seven, or twelve, depending which version you're reading – of her sons or step-sons into swans, leaving their younger sister to years of isolated and silent toil as she weaves the shirts made of nettles that will break the spell and set them free. When she succeeds not only has she won her brothers back, vanquished the spell and with it the Queen but she has also created an adult life for herself, in the form of marriage to a prince (Queendom, again) and motherhood. Once again the young and apparently helpless heroine has won her way through the challenge to maturity. And these are not light challenges; both of these stories contain the threat of death as a very possible outcome.

In the fairytale *The Snow Queen*, young Gerda quests through the seasons of the year in order to find her playmate Kay, whom the Snow Queen has stolen away. By the time Gerda rescues him and melts the splinters of ice that are lodged in his eye and heart with her tears, the two have matured from children to become lovers. In this story Gerda is quite specifically told that she cannot be given any gifts to help defeat the Snow Queen; that what she has, herself (or who she is) must be enough. She risks death at several stages in her journey. Kay himself had not asked to be rescued – in fact, the opposite – and nearly everyone Gerda meets is determined to delay her indefinitely or dissuade her from her quest. But once again a Queen has provided an initiation for Gerda that has seen her mature from a girl into a woman.

There are other fairytales where the role of Queen is played by a witch, such as in *Hansel and Gretel* and *The Little Mermaid*. These stories again have the theme of a young girl's fascination for the older, powerful feminine (evidenced as the compelling allure of the gingerbread cottage, or the desperately desired magic to turn a mermaid into a human with legs and an immortal soul). There is a necessity for the heroine to accept the witch's terms; then thwart her; turn the story around and take that power to free herself. Both girls escape the power of the witch by defying her – Gretel by tricking the witch and pushing her into the oven and the Little Mermaid by refusing to kill the prince she loves – both thus become the powerful feminine force within the story. Gretel saves Hansel and herself and returns home, where their father has got rid of their step-mother (yet another step-mother), who had forced the children out into the forest. The Little Mermaid, more unhappily, dissolves into the sea, then to be lifted into the air and become an air sprite with, indeed, an immortal soul.

This repeated theme of a powerless girl undergoing an apparently impossible challenge and succeeding – and most especially as a transition into adulthood – sounds to me like a meeting with the Dark Goddess. Added to that, these Queens carry all the powers of the Dark Goddess. They hold the powers of life and death (they are often the girl's mother or step-mother, or else a powerful practitioner of magic); as well as many characteristics that are projected, in our world, onto the dark feminine, or sometimes just the powerful feminine. It seems to me these Queens are only one step removed from the Dark Goddess and they are playing out her role of initiator into the power of the feminine.

Early on in Psyche's tale she avoids Aphrodite, asking for help from other Gods and Goddesses. They make it clear to her that the only hope she has is to directly approach the terrifying, all powerful Aphrodite, who wishes her dead. It is not usual to think of Aphrodite as a Dark Goddess, but here she clearly mirrors the attributes of one. And once you have come to the attention of the Dark Goddess, there is no other way through than by submitting to the tasks she sets you and undergoing her initiation, whatever that may be.

Persephone takes on the challenge set her and becomes the Dark Goddess herself; a classic story of a maiden initiated into Queen. Some stories place Hecate as watching or hearing Persephone's disappearance (or abduction) but taking no action. Why did she do nothing to save her, or even tell anyone for a long time where Persephone had gone? I think here is the answer. She was witnessing, or possibly facilitating, an initiation.

These Queens with their dark and terrible powers are busy creating initiations for girls into maturity and power. The feminine forces in these stories are split between two characters, one young, powerless and good (or maybe just innocent); the other older, powerful and even evil. When the younger character integrates the powers of the older, the two forces join together. Beyond the faces of the bright Goddess and the Dark Goddess is the one Goddess. Beyond the polarity of the helpless child Snow White and her wicked step/mother is the mature, integrated Snow White; free, happy and now a Queen. Beyond each of the polarities of these tales – the young girl facing a life-threatening challenge and the Queen who seems to threaten her – is the end of these tales; the main character assuming her adult place in the world and an integration of power and the polarities within herself.

How do we apply this information? We have to understand what the dark feminine forces are in our own lives. Easily I can name menarche, childbirth and menopause as the traditional life/death related moments. But we are not living in a simple world, where such things are acknowledged as initiators into levels of power and understanding. In our world the dark feminine is likely also to manifest in such ways as depression; addiction; being a victim to violence, abuse or circumstance; mental or emotional instability; physical illness. To apply this learning, one then has to say that these huge and frightening forces can be, in fact, initiations. That they can be the gateway into power. That they can be the raw material – indeed, they must be the raw material – for our transition into Queenship, the integration of the powerful and mature feminine. They are the initiation of the Dark Goddess.

As for how to do it – the stories are very clear on this. Look at Gerda, look at Inanna, look at the Little Mermaid or Psyche or the girl with the swan brothers. Not one of these characters will succeed if they do not accept the challenge; a challenge which appears to be impossible. Not one of them has a chance of success unless she follows her heart, what she knows to be right; although usually there is little or no confirmation of this in the world around her.

The Dark Goddess, or the wicked Queen of the fairytales is seen as evil only by our eyes that have been taught to condemn the dark feminine, and most particularly the *power* of the dark feminine. It is hardly surprising that within a patriarchy these young (uninitiated) female characters are inevitably drawn to their powerful, older counterparts. This is perhaps even why we require this initiation/intervention of the 'dark forces'; because we are currently not supported in more orthodox ways to achieve maturity and power. Our culture conspires to keep us youthful, innocent and powerless.

The wicked Queen of many fairytales, supported by Dark Goddess myths, forces the characters into a confrontation which they cannot escape. Although they appear to be losing everything, in fact by the end they have gained their heart's desire, or – put another way – their wholeness and maturity. It seems that there is no way but to accept the challenge demanded of you by the Dark Queen and to follow your heart each step of the way. You can treat the Dark Goddess – or her presentation in your life as depression or whatever – as external to yourself, but it looks awfully like she is actually your own power, that you are disconnected from and must, at any cost, fulfill its terms and integrate.

A SAMPLE ASCENT
How Not To Do It

Only an hour or two after my Descent I started to work on my Ascent. I decided to tackle each gate again. For some reason, probably because I'd been crying too much and couldn't think straight anymore, I tried to do the work of the Ascent in the wrong order – that is starting at the First Gate again; going downwards instead of upwards. This didn't work as a way of emerging from the Underworld, though I did some useful things.

I began with the First Gate, where I had left behind my marriage. I decided to reconnect with other people. I made a list of my seven dearest friends, choosing them by the power of each one's integrity, and their knowledge of and commitment to me. I decided to tell them my terrible fears, that I felt rejected and criticized, forced to retreat to aloneness. I would tell them I could not seem to find a way to work through things.

I wrote emails. I picked up the phone. The friend who answered surprised me with her sympathy and I cried. Over the next few days I received answers, emails, calls; I met one of my friends for coffee. People told me of their own relationship difficulties and pointed me towards resources. I began to feel more stable, more seen and heard.

For the Second Gate I had relinquished my relationship with my son. I knew he would be all right without me, but there were still things he needed from a mother. He needed help with looking into universities; with managing a diary of important dates and deadlines; with learning to drive. I would provide that help. He needed cuddles, love and affection and someone to play card and board games with. I chose to be that person. I stepped into that new phase of my old role and felt a quiet strength in it.

The Third Gate was hard. I decided to analyze my relationship. Before I had been afraid to look at the details; even though I am so good at spotting patterns, at counting; I had been afraid of what it will tell me. But I was past the fear, or living in it fully so I listed my difficulties for the first time. It was terrifying to do and yet it came out really clearly, as if it was just waiting. The difficulties still looked difficult, I couldn't get around that. The positives were a strong balance, but they didn't solve the difficulties. I hoped that, having brought it into the top level of my consciousness, I would begin to work on solutions, or at least express the difficulties. In the past I had refused to admit they existed at all or had any weight to them, so determined was I to stay positive.

I did the Fourth Gate as well, which on the way down was my defenses. It was clear to me I needed some good, supportive resolutions. To make sure I exercised, at least five times a week. To eat three meals a day at proper times. That's always been one of my worst patterns, not eating when I am in a crisis or feel bad about myself and then working myself into a nervous state where I feel ill and fatigued and start physically falling apart; a kind of punishing of the body. I thought surely I could do without that, by now.

Weirdly I forgot the Fifth, Sixth and Seventh Gates. Perhaps I just ran out of time. It stayed there, in my journal, a backwards and incomplete attempt...

How To Actually Do It

Six months later, when I was wondering what happened to me, I came back to it. – Oh! I did a Descent; yes that's right. Oh – I forgot to return? I tried to do an Ascent backwards? I didn't even finish it? Oh well, that explains it –

So I did it again, properly this time. From the bottom up.

Seventh Gate – robe – life. This life, my life. I claim this house – mine. I claim my choices; to live here, with my son, my partner and the cats – mine. I claim the life of a writer, mother, priestess, teacher – mine. I claim wellbeing – physical health, mental calm and stimulation, emotional growth – mine.

Sixth Gate – measuring rod – my understanding. I claim my insights, into my own purposes and the wider picture. I claim comprehension. I understand some of the story of how I came here, and the tasks set in the relationship. I claim knowledge of my own patterns and defenses and where they lead me. I claim acceptance of my current position.

Fifth Gate – armband – status. I claim my persona in the world; the face of me via the web, my workshops, my writing. I claim visibility; vocalization; creativity; individuality; service. I claim my status.

Fourth Gate – breastplate – defenses. I claim again my intellect, my knowledge and my rationality. I claim my emotionalism, my depth, my sensitivity. I claim even my fear and judgment. I claim my calmness, my expansiveness. They are all defenses and sometimes necessary and sometimes positive. I claim them.

Third Gate – beads – order. I claim an order to my days; my lists, achievements, moving though things. I claim an order to my relationship with my son; moving into releasing and relinquishing him. I claim an order with my partner; intimacy, closeness, challenge/hurt, retreat, healing, return. I claim an order in my priorities, and in my lifetime, and in my major tasks. I reclaim order.

Second Gate – jewels – my son. I reclaim my love and joy in him. I reclaim my responsibilities – to him and to the world, in producing him. I reclaim our closeness, mutual understanding, playfulness, empathy and affection. I reclaim my mothering and my relationship to him as mother.

First Gate – crown – marriage. I reclaim my marriage. I reclaim my optimism, my hope, my sense of excitement within it. I reclaim my compassion for us, and my power within the relationship. I reclaim being fully present and I reclaim utilizing resources and support. I reclaim love and trust.

Equinox to Equinox, autumn to spring.

And that version of the Ascent worked.

Dream

I had this dream the night before I was initiated into the rank of High Priestess. I dreamt I went to the ritual and there were many people there, people I was not expecting. It was a bit like a wild party. I did not feel safe, there was a dangerous edge to the air and I began to wonder about ritual sacrifice; I began to wonder about the sanity and motivation of these people, who seemed stranger to me with every minute that passed.

Before I could leave – and we were in a kind of abandoned warehouse out on the edge of nowhere – there was nowhere safe to go, anyway – they took me into another, smaller room with no windows and only one door and stood around me in a circle. It looked very bad. There were maybe ten or twelve of them and they seemed involved in a ritual I had no part in. Something happened – they put a sack over my head, or maybe they cut me with a knife, or I ended up folded into a wooden chest, alive – and my spirit left.

It ran away – so hard and fast it was all I could do to hold onto it, to go with it and not let go the thread. I rose up like a bird, a falcon I thought, straight into the sky. I had a sensation of wings and rapid height and uncontrollable, driving flight. It was like a kite cut loose and because I tracked it, stayed with it, I lost entirely the map of where my body was or how to get back to it. By the time my spirit stilled and slowed I was in deep and utter blackness; the night sky without the stars. I could not tell up from down, or forward from back. I did not know which direction I had come from. I tried to feel for my body – or for the path I had taken, to get here – and there was nothing, no sign or feeling or indication of direction at all. I felt like screaming, though I knew it would have been a silent scream, no sound could be made or heard here. I had nothing – my eyes open or closed made no difference. I could not find my way back.

I thought of my friend, back on earth. I reached out blindly, senselessly to her. *I am so lost I am beyond hope,* I said. *There is no way back.* I heard her voice in my head. *Imagine it,* she said. *Imagine you could find your way back.* So I imagined it, I had nothing better to do. I picked a direction randomly; there was no sense I was guessing it, feeling it, it was utterly random. I began to imagine I was moving in that direction, though movement of any kind seemed both impossible and irrelevant. I tried to imagine the blackness was moving past me, or I was moving through it, though it all stayed entirely the same, with no sensation at all of movement or change. I imagined going faster, traveling at the speed of light; quashing down fears of traveling in any one of a million wrong directions at the speed of light. I painted a small picture for my mind's eye, of my body as I had left it, folded up. I told myself I was traveling towards it, a speck of light returning from the vast blackness.

I began to feel a difference. The darkness was less utterly without sensation, I felt a friction as I passed through it. I did seem to be moving. It got denser but more like a path, less like outer space and more like layers of atmosphere. It occurred to me that if I was moving, I was very unlikely to be heading in the right direction. I did not stop to question this but decided to imagine I was moving even faster.

And then with very little in-between I was suddenly there, above my body which was curled up at the feet of my friend, who was standing in the wasteland, looking up at the sky (and it was daylight, not night) and then I was inside it, my own body. Which felt nearly absurd, how impossible that had been. Literally, it was not possible, what I had done. And then I woke up.

RITUAL: A SEVEN-FOLD ASCENT
The intention of this ritual is to ascend back through the seven gates, reclaiming what you discarded or left behind on your way into the Underworld.

Time: 1 hour +
You will need:
- Journal or a pen and paper
- Your notes from when you did the *Seven-Fold Descent Ritual*
- Optional drawing things
- A safe place – whether it's by the altar in your living room, at a friend's house, a counselor's office, or outside in a place special to you
- Someone to check in and check out with

- Tissues
- Your altar, and/or offering/s to the Dark Goddess, or at least a candle
- If you used seven objects for the Descent, use the same ones for this Ascent
- The *bread and water of life* or representatives
- A mirror

Preparation

This is a companion-piece to the *Seven-Fold Descent* presented on page 99. You may like to remind yourself of the Descent you undertook, especially if it was a week or more ago, by reading through your journal entries. You will be reclaiming the things you relinquished on your way down into the Underworld. These things will have changed – transformed – in their meaning or your relationship to them. They might have strengthened, deepened or they may have fallen away. You may find yourself understanding some of them completely differently.

This is not a stand-alone ritual and should **only** be done after the Descent. The time you leave between the Descent and Ascent is up to you. In Inanna's story it is three days (or three nights, if you are following the moon's cycle). You may have chosen a week or a month.

If you do this Ascent once, but still feel partly held in the Underworld, you can repeat it a week (or more) later.

The Check-In Person

It's good to have someone to process issues with, or share revelations with, or witness any undertakings you commit to as a result of your Ascent. This person can help you to make sure you're grounded after the ritual, to remind you about eating, resting and exercising or other personal things that they know will assist you. If this person is different than your original check-in person, orient them to the process you have already undertaken, as well as to this one. While an Ascent is not generally as challenging as a Descent, it still is part of the same process and should be treated with respect and care.

The Safe Place

Once again, it's important to undertake this ritual in a safe, secure place where you have access to what you need and will not be interrupted. You can do the Ascent in the same place as you did the Descent. If this is not possible, make a link with your earlier ritual through objects you place on your altar and looking back over your earlier notes and drawings.

The Altar

If you still have your Dark Goddess altar you may like to add to it or rearrange it for this ritual. Otherwise, make an altar especially for this ritual. It may be very simple – a cloth with your candle, your bread and water of life, your mirror and an offering – or more complex. Place your bread and water of life on the altar.

Optional – Seven Objects

If you used seven objects in your Descent, you should use the same ones (or as near as possible) in your Ascent.

Recording Your Ascent

I like to make a record as I go back through the gates. Without my notes I might never have realized I attempted this ritual backwards, or that I hadn't finished it. Recording this ritual will help you to remember exactly what happened at each gate and can assist with your map-making, afterwards. If you prefer, you can record the whole thing at the end of the ritual. You may choose to use a form other than journaling; such as drawing, words spoken into a recording device or poetry.

The Ritual

- Begin this ritual by casting a circle, meditating, dancing, chanting or some other way of creating sacred space. If you did not begin the last ritual very formally, you may like to this time, following one of these suggestions.
- Light your candle if you are using one. Other options include sprinkling water mixed with a few drops of essential oil over yourself and the space; sounding chimes or burning incense.
- Making a dedication to, or acknowledgement of the Dark Goddess is a way to focus your thoughts and energy, and to begin reflecting on your experiences in the Underworld. By now you may have quite a specific relationship with her; or she may still be a shadowy figure to you; or you may understand her as a part of yourself. Reflecting on your experience with her, offer her a truthful dedication (or acknowledgement) such as, *I acknowledge the dark as equal with the light*; or, *I dedicate myself to the Dark Goddess for the next three dark moons*; or, *From now on, I will strive to know and integrate the Dark Goddess*. You can write this dedication down on a slip of paper and place it on your altar; you can speak (or sing) it aloud; you can whisper it quietly to yourself or write it in your journal and press it to your heart.
- Let yourself feel again the depths of the Underworld. You might have experienced this most strongly in a ritual, a dream, a real-life experience or a meditation. Summon up the emotions, the visions, the impressions you had of this place. Remember also your encounter with the Dark Goddess. This may have been frightening, exciting, strengthening or challenging. Call up the deep part of you that met with her; and see if anything has changed within you as a result of that meeting.
- If you have an offering for the Dark Goddess, lay it on the

altar.

- If you like, and especially if you have not already done so in another ritual, either taste the bread and water of life from your altar, or sprinkle a few drops and a few crumbs onto yourself.
- If you finished the Descent ritual naked, you can begin this one naked, for continuity.

The Seventh Gate

At the Seventh Gate you surrendered your life; your physical body as well as the life you have lived until now.

To pass up through the Seventh Gate you need to take your life back.

If you are using objects, pick up the object you surrendered at the Seventh Gate (Inanna's object was her robe). Ask yourself how you can represent, to yourself; the taking back of your life. For example if you are using a robe, you might put it on. You might choose to write something down – how you will regard your life from now on, or what you will welcome into your life, or a resolution about your life – or just to dance, wordlessly reclaiming your body and its life.

Imagine yourself as passing through a gateway or over a threshold; or if you like, take one pace forwards.

Before you move on make sure you feel you really have reclaimed your life. This can be hard to achieve in a single ritual, so you can make a list of things you will do (perhaps even with times when you will do them) so that you fully experience reclaiming your life and body. Make them body-related things, such as walking in a forest, baking a cake, or going to a dance class. Then move on to the Sixth Gate.

The Sixth Gate

To pass back through the Sixth Gate you need to reclaim whatever it was you lost or gave up here, on your way down. If you are using objects, pick up the object you left behind at the Sixth Gate (Inanna's object was her measuring rod and line).

Imagine yourself as passing through a gateway or over a threshold; or stand up and take one pace forwards.

What you do next will depend on what you gave up. This was one of the last things you surrendered, and may have been a powerful force in holding you into your previous life. If it was an attribute, you need to find out how it has changed in you (perhaps it has vanished, to be replaced by the unfolding of a different attribute). If it was a relationship, or a part of your life, check how your attitude to it has changed, as a result of being in the Underworld. Be aware of exactly what you are taking back and how it has transformed.

You may need to take further actions – perhaps after you have finished the ritual – to put this fully in place. For example, you may need to change how you behave in relation to another person (your mother, your boss, your friend); to rework the way you carry out some aspect of your life or to make a resolution to yourself or another. At the very least make a note of any completions that are required for the Sixth Gate, before you move on. Then continue to the Fifth Gate.

The Fifth Gate

To pass back through the Fifth Gate you need to reclaim whatever it was you gave up here, on your way down. If you are using objects, pick up the object you surrendered at the Fifth Gate (Inanna's object was her armband).

Depending on what you gave up at this gate find some way to represent reclaiming it, being aware that it has probably changed form. Maybe you don't even want it back, and you are reclaiming, instead, something more essential or a need you have been ignoring. If you laid down something like your dreams or ambitions, you might like to recover them, and remind yourself of what they are; they may seem closer to you now or more real.

If you gave up a quality you have longed to embody, revisit that quality and ask yourself if that is still what you desire. You may find you have it already, or that it is no longer relevant to you, or that it has been replaced by something else.

Imagine yourself as passing through the gateway or over a threshold. If you prefer you can literally take a step forwards.

You can take a few moments to write down what you learn; to embody it through stretching, sounding or dance; or just to lie quietly, breathing it in. Feel how you will be in the world, when you return bearing this attribute. Then progress on to the Fourth Gate.

The Fourth Gate

To return through the Fourth Gate you need to take back whatever it was you surrendered here, on your way down. If you are using objects, pick up the object you placed down at the Fourth Gate (Inanna's object was her breastplate).

Remember what it was you relinquished here; perhaps some part of your defenses or your achievements or personality. Revisit it now, to see how it has transformed while you were in the Underworld. Perhaps you will welcome it back, or perhaps your understanding or need of it has radically changed.

One way to integrate this is to draw a picture of yourself showing what it is you are taking back. Even if you don't consider yourself someone who can draw, a visual representation can be very powerful and evocative.

See yourself passing through a gateway or over the threshold; or stand up and take one pace forwards.

If there are any actions you need to take, to consolidate this gate, make a note of them in your journal. If it's a resolution about your future behavior, write it down. If you feel you need some time to assimilate, take it now and drink some water, stretch or rest for five minutes. Then pass onto the Third Gate.

The Third Gate

To pass up through the Third Gate you need to take back whatever it was you gave up, on your way down. If you are using objects, pick up the object you placed down at the Third Gate (Inanna's object was her double strand of beads).

Remembering what you gave up here, think what it means to take it back into your life. This was probably something very precious to you, that was hard to let go of; but its meaning may have changed for you since then. You may have a completely different relationship now to what you gave up, and you may take it back into your life on very different terms. If you need to spend some time processing this, do so. Make notes in your journal, or simply write how it was for you before, and how it is now. There may be further action that you wish or need to take, to fully integrate this thing back into your life. Make a note of what you will do (and when you will do it).

Pass through this gate or over the threshold, either in your mind or literally, taking a step.

When you are ready, move on to the Second Gate.

The Second Gate

To pass up through the Second Gate you need to take back whatever it was you gave up, on your way down. If you are using objects, pick up the object you placed down at the Second Gate (Inanna's object was her necklet).

You may feel exalted as this process continues, or overwhelmed or empowered. You may feel grief, fear or excitement at the way your life seems to be changing, or you may feel frustration at the immensity and difficulty of it. Breathe deeply and focus on the Second Gate. Whatever it was you gave up here was something of immense importance to you. Revisit this and ask yourself in what way you are reclaiming it; how you will build it back into your life, or move on from it.

This may call for an attitude change, or for direct actions such as writing a letter to someone; learning further communication skills; developing a spiritual practice or confronting a problem in your life. Make sure you record this, and how you feel about it in your journal. If you want to write down any special resolutions or understandings, do so.

When you feel you have completed this for now, imagine yourself passing through the gateway or over a threshold; or if you like, take one pace forwards. Then move onto the First Gate.

The First Gate

To return through the First Gate, back into the upper world, you need to take back whatever it was you gave up here on your way down. If you are using objects, pick up the object you placed down at the First Gate (Inanna's object was her crown).

What you gave up at the First Gate is quite probably what motivated you to visit the Underworld in the first place. Taking it back may be nearly as emotional as giving it up. It's possible you will have completely changed in your orientation to it. You may be taking it back only symbolically, as you have already moved beyond it, or its form has changed so radically as to be a different thing now. Sometimes we discover the things we have clung to exist very differently to how we have imagined them, and we have to completely change our understandings, our actions and our emotional relationships to parts of our lives. This can be very challenging.

You may not be able to complete all the integration you need for this right away. Even as you experienced loss and grief in giving it up, you may also experience these things when you take it back into your life, in its changed form or as you now view it. Perhaps there are further actions you will need or wish to take, to assist you in this integration. If you have ideas of what these actions may be, make a note of them. It is likely that this integration will play out over a period of time and even though it may feel immense right now, usually in the non-ritual world changes take a while to implement.

Then imagine yourself passing through this final gate, or over a threshold. If you like, stand up and take a pace forwards.

- Once you have come through all seven gates, you are back in the upper world. You might like to drink some water, do a breathing exercise or make a record of the ritual in your journal.
- Before you finish this process entirely, look in the mirror. Look for the integration of the Dark Goddess within you, and acknowledge that she is a part of yourself, and of each person. See if you can find some connection with your soul, that deep part of you that you quested into the Underworld for. Offer yourself thanks, for all you have done and what you will continue to do, as you live out the truths and understandings you have discovered.
- To complete, or ground a ritual, you should do all of the things you did to begin it, in the reverse order. You can dismantle or pack up your altar – or if you are leaving it there, blow out any candles and put out any incense that is burning. Now ground or bring to completion your circle or sacred space. Finally you can do something to symbolize that the space you have used for your ritual is now ordinary space again – make a tone, or chime, or stamp your feet and wave your arms around.
- Remember to connect with your check-in person, to tell them you have completed the ritual. If you don't feel like discussing it in depth, make a time in the next few days to talk with them more deeply. If for some reason you did *not* complete the ritual, set a time for doing that and let your check-in person know when it is. The more powerful this ritual is for you, the more important it is to complete it.

INTEGRATING YOUR JOURNEY TO THE DARK GODDESS

There is no way to be alive and avoid pain and difficulty. Even if we lead a blameless life illness, death and misfortune occur. Logically we know and accept this. Our experience of these things is what enables us, later, to reach out to friends, family or even strangers who are suffering, and to be proactive when a community or place is threatened. Our children will have fears, nightmares, illnesses and unguessable difficulties as they grow up. If we had never been through any of that, how could we help them? If we did not know what it was to suffer physical pain, how could we begin to understand the lives of those who are suffering it? If we had never experienced emotional pain – the ending of a relationship, the death of a loved one, a failure where we wished for success – how could we relate to others in emotional turmoil?

If we really examine our lives and the times we have had of insight, understanding and deepening we will find a significant number of those growth times have occurred after – and even as a direct result of – a trauma, depression or a fallow period. Further, if we look for times of complete bliss, of oneness with the universe or of ecstatic communion with the divine, we find that at least some of those times have occurred when we have been in places of great loss, trauma and darkness. While we were in the Underworld. The times when we have known ourselves the most deeply, truly and inspiredly were rarely when we felt on top of the pyramid, surfing success but rather when we were at the bottom, in the depths and eye to eye with the Dark Goddess.

It seems that not only must we submit to this round of pain and growth, but also admit that it is, ultimately, good for us. That darkness contains the seeds of some of the best and brightest things; that indeed the light can be best perceived in the darkest places. The ability and willingness to offer genuine support to other people in times of need is no small thing, either. And compassion, this *feeling with* another – well, some of us have good imaginations; but most of us have been there, ourselves. So can we validate our own times of darkness, these journeys to the Dark Goddess as not just inevitable, but valuable? Irreplaceable? Can we acknowledge they offer us something we would never receive if we managed to stay in the light all the time? And, understanding this, can we learn not to suffer so much in them; or even to meet times of Descent with not just recognition but an embrace?

Take me down, I will follow you gladly.

This is not to imagine we would welcome trauma, difficulty and pain but that, recognizing it, we would be grateful to submit to a process we know – from reading the myths, and from watching others and from our past experience – will take us through. I can't say I've reached this place myself. I am more of the *take a deep breath and jump* school. That is; I recognize it, I know I have to go there and once I've admitted that, I try to go as fast as possible, in the optimistic belief that it will be over sooner. I am assisted by the knowledge that the pain of postponing the Descent is an added extra I don't need.

For myself, and many of the women I've talked to, there's a sense of having lived most of one's whole life in the Underworld. For us it may seem there is more down than up, or even that there is no up. While this may serve as a counter-balance for all those people who adamantly refuse to go down, at all; or those who resist as fiercely as humanly possible, it is not the pattern of the moon and the seasons. That pattern has distinct phases, and equal time is given to the different phases. If you are someone who feels held in the Underworld, detained there beyond the length of an ordinary Descent (if there is any such thing) you may need to work to consciously rebalance the time you spend in the Underworld and your dedication – even if unconscious or apparently unwilling – to the Dark Goddess.

I've known many women who felt they were dedicated to the Dark Goddess. Women who suffered through abuse and/or incest in their childhoods, and however hard they've fought to get free, still feel eternally marked by that experience, bound to the darkness. And women who've spent their working lives helping others, whether in nursing, addiction counseling, in women's refuges, working with abused children or similar jobs; who feel the Dark Goddess an overwhelming and unavoidable presence. There are women, also, who have experienced a string of deaths and traumas – debilitating illnesses or recurring depression; children who become addicts, die young or are severely disabled; partners who die or disappear – who cannot seem to shake free from an unending stream of disaster in their personal lives. Some of these women also feel that the Dark Goddess has them under her thumb.

There's no easy answer for any of this. There may be one or two balancing factors. One is in understanding that our culture's wholesale determination to eternally remain in, and only cohort with the light creates a build up where those of us who give any room, at all, to darkness may find ourselves swamped not just by a personal backlog (though there's that, as well), but by a cultural and societal backlog. Energetically, it may be that as soon as we individually declare a willingness to deal with the dark as well as the light, we are overwhelmed; the barriers down and the floodwaters loosed. This may also (sometimes) be a misjudgment on our part – we are so used to wanting and expecting everything to be lightness, that even a portion of darkness can be overwhelming; it can feel like eighty percent even if it's probably more like forty percent.

To get to the place of welcoming it, I have started small. I have started by welcoming night, sleep, the dark moon, winter. I welcome the down-time that comes after overwhelm; the recovery period after a sickness. Now my goal is to get to that place where I am not just welcoming it because of its benefits to me AFTER I survive it, but for itself. I believe that no one part of that four-part process of preparing to descend, descending, being in the Underworld and ascending is more significant, valuable or sacred than any other part. So if I was not attached to some parts being preferable to other parts; I would not suffer so much in the parts I currently don't like. If I considered them all genuinely, equally interesting, rewarding and meaningful I would be valuing all of my life. I would be valuing the Dark Goddess.

We are creatures of light and dark. We know the power of the moon and stars, and that of the sun. We acknowledge summer and also winter. We dream our inner mysteries and we dance our celebrations. We live in the upper world with our jobs, relationships and families and we live also in the Underworld, in our souls with the depths of our truths, and our yearnings and potential. We transit from one to the other, continually. We seek to integrate these states and we know it is a work in progress, always. Living eternally in the dark is no more a natural existence than staying eternally in the light. The integration and wholeness come as we journey back and forth; at least some of the time willingly. And as the way becomes more known to us we make maps. We share the findings of those maps with others and we use them to deepen our understanding each time we travel those paths.

The Dark Goddess is in essence a mystery; as is the nature of our souls. We can visit her, in the realm that is her own. We will be gifted with insight, with understanding, with compassion and with new life. The challenges will always be to integrate these understandings into our daylit lives; and to return again, seemingly facing the loss of all we have accrued, for yet deeper versions of ourselves to emerge. The Dark Goddess is the deep well we draw from. Hers is the Eye of Death and hers the ability to give birth anew. She is utterly ferocious and unending compassion and time spent with her teaches us those qualities. A journey to the Dark Goddess is a sacred endeavor to visit the depths of your soul, and arise reborn.

MAKING A MAP OF THE JOURNEY

Now you have completed the cycle of the journey to the Dark Goddess it's great to record it, to finish making your map. For this fourth part of your mapping you might like to include references to the earlier three stages – Preparing to Descend, Descending and In the Underworld – or you may prefer to focus solely on your Ascent. There are some suggestions below, but of course you should not limit yourself to those; you might want to create an opera, decorate a kite or design and make a piece of jewelry.

After you've finished all four pieces of your map consider showing them; either to friends, your women's circle or publicly in some way. You may choose to publish some of your writing as a blog or article; you may choose to enter a piece or more in a local art exhibition or put photos of your work up on the internet. What you have created is a rare, vital and valuable thing; a map of a conscious journey to the Underworld, and its return. Treasure it.

Journaling

Your journal can contain many other things as well as your written record of processes and rituals. You can stick in photos or pictures (or draw them, of course); as well as bits and pieces left over from rituals such as ribbons, tokens, leaves and ashes. You can put in poems or quotes from other sources; list songs or books that have been especially helpful or inspiring and write down resolutions, processes you have tried (or ones you'd like to try) and significant conversations. You can free-write on issues that are in your life, or dream up a five year plan for yourself. If you are journaling this part of your map include any significant stages you noticed in your Ascent out of the Underworld. Make sure to include your new insights and the changes you see happening in and around you.

Mural

Perhaps you like really big maps? Do you have a spare wall, or an old sheet or length of canvas that can be turned into a mural? Make your design bold, to cover a large space. Perhaps you will paint a literal map of the seven gates of Ascent, or a series of impressions, or complex images and symbols. You can work in color, or stay in black and white for a stark visual effect. You can include words – pieces of poetry or key phrases – and use metallic silver or gold paint for emphasis. Allow your experiences as you ascended from the Underworld to come through in form, color and design.

Fabric Work – Quilting, Embroidery, Weaving...

Using whatever fabric working techniques you like, make a ritual robe to wear. Or make a wall-hanging or a bedcover or a veil. Use quilting, embroidery, weaving, bead-work, screen printing, patchwork, felting, appliqué or anything else you can think of.

Create a piece that expresses the feelings you experienced during your Ascent. Put in references to the gifts you received from the Underworld; and, if you like, a symbol for any significant thing you felt you lost, finished or left behind when you made your Ascent. Wear or display your fabric work with pride... or keep it in a special chest... or frame it... or tuck it away for your next ritual.

AFTERWORD: THE CYCLE CONTINUES

Of the many women I know who do this journeying to the Dark Goddess there is one, just one who greets her with open arms, as a sister. Who truly smiles at her presence, laughs aloud at her revelations and anticipates with joy the sweeping changes she will bring.

It is my ambition to raise the number of those women who greet the arrival of the Dark Goddess this way to two. It is my ambition to raise that number to twenty. To a hundred. To a thousand and a thousand thousand. The Dark Goddess is part of our essence, part of the deep powerful feminine force of life and death. She is part of who we are – and who we can become – both in our most private selves and out in the world. The Dark Goddess is the caretaker of our souls.

The journey to the Dark Goddess does not stop after one Descent and Ascent. It is periodic and even continual; seeking to weave itself into the basic patterns of our lives. Each time we descend we let go of the old parts of our lives, each time in the Underworld we revisit the truth of our soul and each time as we ascend we integrate some of the gifts of the Dark Goddess. Like a snake in a fresh skin, emerged we spend a while shiny and sleek before that skin, too, becomes old and we start to rub up against the roughness of life, seeking to slough it off. Each time we undertake this journey – especially when we undertake it consciously – we receive further opportunities for diving deep within ourselves, for approaching the mysteries, seeking truth and coming closer to our soul and its guardian, the Dark Goddess.

There exist many different tools and approaches to integrating these revealed aspects of ourselves into our lives. There are mythic, or spiritual approaches, such as the work of following the paths outlined in the stories of Gods, Goddesses, heroes and heroines; or through prayer and devotion. There are psychological approaches including analysis, cognitive behavioral therapy and counseling; and self-help approaches such as support groups, work-books and inner reflection. Some of the books listed in the resources section at the end of this book may be helpful to you, and many others exist.

If you have come across a significant problem, or difficulty in your life (which may have remained unchanged throughout your entire Descent, time in the Underworld and Ascent) it is time to seek outside help. I recommend finding a counselor you can speak openly to. You may have to try several. Counseling can also be a type of Underworld journey, as you begin to look at issues that have been hidden or not clearly understood and eventually take actions to bring your life into a place of greater ease and synchronicity with who you really are and what is most important to you. There can be many challenges along the way but when you bring the Dark Goddess along as an ally, she can make a significant difference to your ability to look at such truths and make changes.

The myths of Persephone, of Inanna and Psyche call out to women. Others as well – among them those of Isis and Mary Magdalene and Cerridwen – seem to draw us in with their shifting of light and shade, their hinting at the mysteries of not just the Dark Goddess but the balance between light and dark. They speak of the initiation of the spirit and the maturation of the feminine. Inanna's story is fascinating because of Ereshkigal; it is Ereshkigal who gives it focus, motivation and resolution. Persephone's story would be nothing if she returned to her mother the same as she departed. Psyche's story is a tale of such extreme endeavor because a Goddess went up against her, and eventually she won through to that same divine level.

The Dark Goddess is both the reason and solution for these stories. And to look at our own lives… we must surely discover that same pattern; that our vitality, our individual sparks of brilliance, what is best and truest about us is born from the dark. Is what remains when everything else is stripped away. Our integrity with our selves – with the whole of ourselves – rests on the basis of our relationship to the Dark Goddess. Without this relationship the light Goddess is half a thing. Without this bonding, and renewal of knowledge of our own soul we become hollow; we are compromised in the essence of our beings and we cease to be our true selves. This is the work the Dark Goddess does and this is the nature of journeying towards her, of meeting her and journeying back.

To embrace the dark and all it represents would be, I believe, a major step forward on the path of – not just reconciliation with the Dark Goddess – but a true embracing of her beauty. There is darkness, and there is light; one follows the other forever. To be at peace with all below; all that is hidden, dark, the Underworld, is to encounter the soul. The Dark Goddess strips away whatever stands between us and this truth. She reminds us that this process – and she herself – is not malicious in intent towards us, but innocent. This is her nature. The Dark Goddess does not exist to teach us lessons but simply, she exists and when we walk forward on our journey that encompasses both dark and light, we walk with her.

Dream

I had a dream that I was part of a school of priestesses who lived in a large building with many rooms. We were engaged in making complex magic, to maintain the threads of life on earth. On the other side of the building was a shadow building, a duplicate, where other priestesses lived in another realm; the darkness. We were dedicated to the light and they, to the dark. We could feel them there, beyond the walls. And every time, every single time we did a magical working – or they did – we had to enter into the space *between*, and once anyone was *between* there was no saying whether she would emerge into the light side or the dark side. That was part of working magic – to undertake that risk of the totality of loss – of place and comrades and personality. Because once you were on the other side no-one could say what would happen, or who you would become, or if you would ever return. And – if you ever did return – you might not be recognizable.

And we did it, and they did it. Even in the magnitude of fear there was sisterhood and a grim understanding of the necessity to face the loss of everything, every time. We worked magic, not knowing. We entered into *between* again and again and sometimes some of them arrived in our house and we did not know them and made room for them, as our sisters. Sometimes some of us disappeared and we knew they were there. And after a while, I realized I, myself, was no longer certain which side I was on or who I had become. But I kept working and they kept working, and I couldn't tell the difference between us, anymore.

RESOURCES

Books on the Dark Goddess

Dancing in the Flames: The Dark Goddess in the Transformation of Consciousness, Marion Woodman and Elinor Dickson. Shambhala, 1997

The Dark Goddess: Dancing with the Shadow, Marcia Starck and Gynne Stern. Crossing Press, 1993

Descent to the Goddess: A Way of Initiation for Women, Sylvia Brinton Perera. Inner City Books, 1981

Kissing the Hag: The Dark Goddess and the Unacceptable Nature of Women, Emma Restall Orr. O-Books, 2009

Mysteries of the Dark Moon: The Healing Power of the Dark Goddess, Demetra George. HarperOne, 1992

Uncursing the Dark: Treasures from the Underworld, Betty De Shong Meador. Chiron Publications, 1992

Books on Myth, Related to the Dark Goddess

Awakening Osiris: The Egyptian Book of the Dead, Normandi Ellis. Red Wheel/Weiser, 2009

Inanna, Queen of Heaven and Earth: Her Stories and Hymns from Sumer, Diane Wolkstein and Samuel Noah Kramer. Harper Perennial, 1983

Life's Daughter/Death's Bride: Inner Transformations through the Goddess Demeter/Persephone, Kathie Carlson. Shambhala, 1997

The Long Journey Home: Re-visioning the Myth of Demeter and Persephone for Our Time, edited by Christine Downing. Shambhala, 2001

Psyche's Seeds: The 12 Sacred Principles of Soul-Based Psychology, Jacquelyn Small. Tarcher Putnam, 2001

Psyche's Sisters: Re-Imagining the Meaning of Sisterhood, Christine Downing. Spring Journal, 2007

She: Understanding Feminine Psychology, Robert A. Johnson.

Harper Paperbacks, 1989

Books on Working with the Dark

Dark Moon Mysteries: Wisdom, Power, and Magic of the Shadow World, Timothy Roderick. New Brighton Books, 2003

Dreaming the Dark: Magic, Sex, and Politics, Starhawk. Beacon Press, 1997

Sisters of the Dark Moon: 13 Rituals of the Dark Goddess, Gail Wood. Llewellyn Publications, 2001

The Women's Wheel of Life: Thirteen Archetypes of Woman at Her Fullest Power, Elizabeth Davis and Carol Leonard. Penguin, 1997

Self Help Books Related to the Dark

The Courage to Heal: A Guide for Women Survivors of Child Sexual Abuse, Ellen Bass and Laura Davis. Harper Paperbacks, 2008

Guidance from the Darkness: The Transforming Power of the Divine Feminine in Difficult Times, The Reverend Mary Murray Shelton. Tarcher Putnam, 2000

In the Meantime: Finding Yourself and the Love You Want, Iyanla Vanzant. Fireside, 1999

Loving What Is: Four Questions That Can Change Your Life, Byron Katie with Stephen Mitchell. Three Rivers Press, 2003

The Shadow Effect: Illuminating the Hidden Power of Your True Self, Deepak Chopra, Marianne Williamson and Debbie Ford. HarperOne, 2011

Other Related Books

The Mythic Path: Discovering the Guiding Stories of Your Past - Creating a Vision for Your Future, David Feinstein and Stanley Krippner. Elite Books, 2006

The Northern Lights Trilogy: Northern Lights, Subtle Knife, Amber Spyglass, (fiction), Philip Pullman. Scholastic, 2008

The Twelve Wild Swans: A Journey to the Realm of Magic, Healing, and Action, Starhawk and Hilary Valentine. HarperOne, 2001

Fiction on the Dark Goddess

At the Back of the North Wind, George MacDonald. First published in 1871. Everyman's Library, 2001

The Earth Witch, Louise Lawrence. Ace Books, 1986

The Eye of the Night, Pauline J. Alama. Spectra, 2002

A Fistful of Sky, Nina Kiriki Hoffman. Ace, 2004

The Jigsaw Woman, Kim Antieau. iUniverse, 2002

The Moon Under Her Feet, Clysta Kinstler. HarperOne, 1991

Ombria in Shadow, Patricia A. McKillip. Ace Trade, 2003

Queen of Swords (play), Judy Grahan. Published in *The Judy Grahan Reader*, Aunt Lute Books, 2009

Sister Light, Sister Dark, Jane Yolen. Tor Teen, 2011

The Spell of Rosette, Kim Falconer. Harper, 2009

Non-Book Resources

The Cave of Elders (CD), Carolyn Hilliyer. Seventh Wave Music. Available at www.seventhwavemusic.co.uk

The Charge of the Star Goddess, originally written by Doreen Valiente. Various versions available on the internet.

The Descent of Inanna: A Guided Journey Through the Ancient Sumerian Goddess Myth (CD), Jalaja Bonheim. Available at www.jalajabonheim.com

Inanna (DVD), Diane Wolkstein, music by Geoffrey Gordon. Available at www.dianewolkstein.com

Listening to Ereshkigal, track on *Aphrodite's Temple* (CD), Jane Meredith. Available at www.janemeredith.com

The Shadow Effect, a movie: Illuminating the Hidden Power of Your True Self (DVD), Deepak Chopra, Marianne Williamson and Debbie Ford. Available at www.amazon.com

ABOUT THE AUTHOR

Jane Meredith is a Priestess of the Goddess. She lives in Australia and works internationally. Jane's book, *Aphrodite's Magic: Celebrate and Heal Your Sexuality* is also published by O-Books. Her workshops include *Journey to the Dark Goddess*, *Tasting the Pomegranate: Persephone's Journey*, and *Descent into Love: the Journey of Psyche*. Jane is passionate about ritual and mythology, magical living and the evocation of the divine. Some of her favorite things are trees, books, dark chocolate and cats.

Jane Meredith's website is: www.janemeredith.com
She has a blog at: www.janemeredith.com/blog
You can sign up for her e-zine or contact Jane at:
jane@janemeredith.com

Moon Books invites you to begin or deepen your encounter with Paganism, in all its rich, creative, flourishing forms.